How wonderful it is that nobody need wait a

single moment before starting to improve the world.

ANNE FRANK

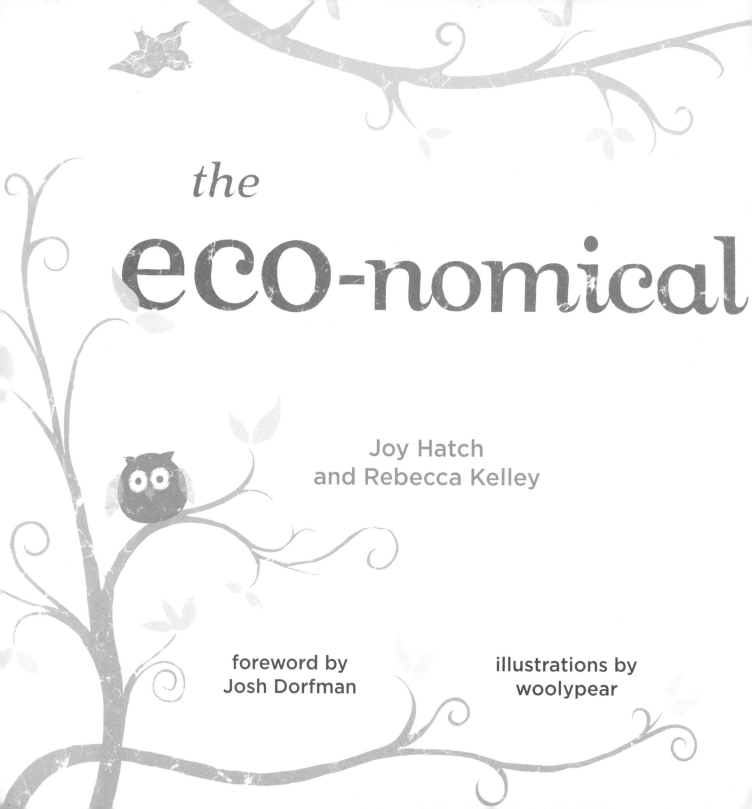

the
eco-nomical

Joy Hatch
and Rebecca Kelley

foreword by
Josh Dorfman

illustrations by
woolypear

**Down-to-Earth Ways for Parents
to Save Money and the Planet**

baby guide

Stewart, Tabori & Chang
NEW YORK

Contents

Foreword

Today we live in a society where the green message is ubiquitous. We turn on "Oprah" and other daytime television shows and watch as numerous green experts offer tips on how to lead more earth-friendly lifestyles. We follow along as a long list of celebrities such as Leonardo DiCaprio, Cameron Diaz, and Brad Pitt appear on camera to make their public case for addressing climate change. Major magazines offer green advice columns and reviews of the latest green products. Talk radio pundits fill the airwaves with their personal views on the need for environmental legislation. If we're to take pundits like Thomas Friedman at their word, "Green," it seems, "has gone mainstream."

But if green has gone mainstream, why is it that when my brother and his wife recently had their first baby, the best I could convince them to do in the name of the environment and the health of my newborn niece was to paint her bedroom using low-VOC (Volatile Organic Compounds) paints that avoid many of the toxins found in conventional paints. Though I run an eco-friendly furniture company, I didn't even suggest that they purchase a crib or other baby furnishings made using eco-friendly materials and non-toxic finishes. I didn't do so for two reasons: 1) I didn't want to be perceived as nagging them in the name of the environment because I find that it's usually counterproductive to do so, and 2) even at my own wholesale price, the eco-friendly furniture I could offer them was still more expensive than the conventional options that they eventually purchased from a well-known national chain.

My experience with my brother and his wife raises important questions for the environmental movement and for all activists—be they authors, business leaders, community organizers, Sierra Club members or Greenpeace volunteers —who are trying to help solve global warming and other pressing environmental challenges. First, how do you really convince people to take environmental action? Second, once people are convinced that action is necessary, how do you most effectively present them with information to act upon?

To the first question, I've found that the best way to convince people to make environmentally conscious decisions is to frame such choices in terms of their own personal self-interest. To take the example of my brother and his wife, I was able to convince them to choose eco-friendly, low-VOC paints because— all environmental considerations aside—it would help keep their baby healthy. And while these paints are typically more expensive than conventional paints, the cost differential was relatively negligible given the small size of their daughter's room. To the second question, I've found that people respond best to environmental information when it's presented in a positive, proactive manner that helps people feel good about the green steps they do take rather than feel bad about the green steps they don't.

This is precisely where *The Eco-nomical Baby Guide* comes in. What distinguishes this book from other green baby books is its emphasis on easy, practical, and realistic steps that new and expecting parents can choose when deciding how to care for their child. Rebecca and Joy also recognize that—contrary to many market research studies—when it comes right down to in-the-aisle shopping decisions, most people are not willing to pay a premium for earth-friendly products. However, instead of being constrained by this insight, the authors still provide a wealth of information about cutting-edge green products, tips, and strategies to reduce the overall cost of child rearing even when compared to conventional child rearing. Without access to such well-gleaned and thoughtful advice, parents may find that even small children can create a very large environmental footprint. But with Rebecca and Joy as your guides, you will learn how going green can serve your self-interest by improving the quality of your and your child's life without sacrificing comfort or convenience and with a mindful eye toward reining in costs.

— Josh Dorfman

Preface

Just a few years ago we stood in your shoes: preparing to welcome our babies and wanting to go green on a limited budget. But where to start? We worried about using cloth diapers, wondered how we could afford eco-friendly products, and panicked when faced with a blank registry list. Since we were both pregnant at the same time, we leaned on each other for green inspiration and information. Even though we had the support of our friendship, well-intentioned friends and family claimed we would never be able to handle the difficulty of caring for baby while conserving resources and cutting costs.

After our babies were born and we put our ideals into action, we began to wonder if we should let people in on our secret: We endured very little hardship and possess only average amounts of determination. It occurred to us that the hard part isn't living green on a dime, it's finding information and support. When our pregnant friends came to us for advice, we realized there was no baby book in print that offered current, real-world tips for living green on a budget. So with spit-up on our shoulders, cloth diapers in the washer, and our babies gurgling in the background, we began writing this book. We recorded everything we had learned and researched what we wished we had known to create an eco-friendly, budget-friendly resource for new parents. *The Eco-nomical Baby Guide* aspires to provide the same benefits we've enjoyed from our friendship: practical advice on parenting matters that make a difference for our planet.

Acknowledgments

Many thanks to all of our early readers for encouraging us through draft after draft (many of which were practically unreadable): Pauli Amornkul, Elizabeth Dorway, Valerie Gallic, Gina Kelley, Amy Pangilinan, Valerie Perrott, Christi Richardson, Abby Schmidt, Kari Smit, and Eileen Spillman. We also appreciated Marie Sherlock's guidance in the early stages of our project. Dozens of friends and family offered their support at several points throughout our long journey to publication; we couldn't have written this without all of you!

We're grateful to our agent, Judith Riven, for her advice and encouragement—and for finding us a home with Stewart, Tabori and Chang. We enjoyed collaborating with our editors, Dervla Kelly and Jennifer Levesque, who helped us fine-tune our writing and embraced the project from the beginning.

And last but not least, we'd like to thank our husbands, Jett Nilprabhassorn and Andrew Henroid, for putting up with the frantic phone calls and frenzied nights of writing and revising. We're especially indebted to Jett for hours of proposal layout, for designing our Web site logo, and for thinking of our title—all voluntarily.

1

Welcoming Baby to a Greener World

Bathing baby in recycled rainwater, stirring cauldrons of pureed peas, fashioning tiny garments out of burlap—is this what it takes to raise an eco-baby on a budget? Hardly! In fact, the tips and insider tricks you'll learn in *The Eco-nomical Baby Guide* will save you time and money while actually simplifying your life.

What *is* an "eco-nomical" baby guide, you ask? Let us set things straight: This is not your grandma's baby guide. Well, not quite, anyway. *The Eco-nomical Baby Guide: Down-to-Earth Ways for Parents to Save Money and the Planet* is packed with commonsense wisdom from previous generations that's been adapted to the age of flushable diapers and Energy Star appliances. So yes—we love our cloth diapers, but we'll launder them in our front-loading washers instead of spending hours wringing them out in a washtub. We've been known to puree our own pumpkin—but we also know where to find the best prices on organic jarred food. No matter what your time or budget constraints may be, we'll offer plenty of options that work for the challenge of raising baby.

Having a child is a fulfilling experience, but let's face it—it comes with economic and environmental difficulties. Along with having anxieties about rising family expenses, many parents are worried about the health of the planet as they welcome their babies into the world. But is it really possible to save money while going green? Not only is it possible, it's actually . . . fun! Far from being a hardship, eco-friendly living on the cheap can be a great adventure. We both get small thrills out of all the ordinary things we do to save money while saving the planet.

Take Joy, for example. Pregnant with her first child, she scoured Craigslist to create the perfect hand-me-down nursery. She managed to find carloads of loot to furnish and decorate her son's room—all for free. Little Roscoe may not have had a $5,000 crib or completely color-coordinated organic crib sheets, but he'll grow up with more money in his college fund and a lighter footprint on the planet.

And then there's Rebecca's somewhat obsessive relationship with cloth diapers. She challenged herself to shell out as little as possible on diapering her baby girl—and ended up spending only $250 for the 2.5 years her daughter was in diapers. She also kept her trash bills low: from birth to potty training, Audrey went through just six packs of disposable diapers and two packages of disposable wipes.

Frugality allows both of us to model what we really value for our children (quality time, relationships, and family) over what we are sometimes pressured to purchase (all the "must-have" baby gear on the market). Armed with *The Eco-nomical Baby Guide*, you'll make greener consumer choices that will keep your baby in style without eating into your savings account.

In the midst of tough economic times, many families are being forced into rather than choosing to live a frugal lifestyle. Still, whether your financial situation requires thrift or not, living with less can have huge benefits for your brood and the environment. It may allow you to cut back your hours at work, go on more family vacations, fund your child's college education, or help you retire just a bit earlier. Plus, you'll prevent your youngster from being saddled with an extra heap of waste in the landfill.

No matter how eco-conscious or penny-wise we are, we could all stand to go just a tad bit greener and add to our arsenal of budgeting skills. In truth there is a little bit of an environmentalist—and an anti-environmentalist—in everyone. By the same token, everyone has an inner tightwad regularly battling the inner consumer. *The Eco-nomical Baby Guide* will offer options that can bring you closer to your own definition of balance. You might not have the skill, the time, or the desire to fashion your own baby booties out of rags, but you can spend money on clothes made out of sustainable materials. Or perhaps you won't go for an organic onesie but instead buy a name-brand garment from a secondhand shop. You may still want a few conventional baby items, but you'll choose to select top-quality products that will last for years and take care to pass them along when your baby is finished using them. All of these choices fall somewhere along the "shades of green" spectrum—and many will save you money, too.

While this book will offer easy, painless eco-friendly options—like greener disposable diapers—it won't hesitate to highlight the kookier ones, too—like infant potty training. You never know what might work for you and your situation until you learn about it and give it a whirl.

Putting the "Eco" in "Eco-nomical"

With eco-friendly baby products pouring onto the market, organic foods crowding grocery store shelves, and sustainability Web sites springing up on the Internet, there has never been a better time to practice green parenting in America. According to a July 2007 article in the *New York Times*, approximately 35 million Americans regularly purchase earth-friendly products, and that number is on the rise. You may be a part of this movement or may be eager to join as your baby's arrival approaches.

Your decision to go green may be more focused on your baby's health than on the well-being of the planet. Some parents worry about dangerous chemicals in baby's immediate environment. *The Eco-nomical Baby Guide* provides current information about the latest on safer plastics, discusses concerns over toys imported from China, and recommends low-cost eco-friendly alternatives. Rather than overwhelming you with lists of toxins lurking in your home, we'll highlight the biggest offenders and reveal the best bargains on safer, greener baby products, from glass bottles to organic wool mattresses.

And what about global warming? News reports of melting glaciers, overfilling land-fills, and disappearing wildlife might have you rushing out to hug a tree—or hide your head in the sand. As new parents, we like the idea of welcoming our babies into a greener world—a world with clean air to breathe and water to drink. But what can we do about it? You may find yourself falling anywhere on the spectrum of "green," from the stridently environmental to the downright apathetic.

A Spectrum of Green Parents

EXTRAORDINARILY GREEN

You grow your own organic produce, operate a solar-powered dryer (i.e., clothesline), and ride your bicycle whenever possible. You literally get goose bumps when you imagine how exciting it would be to start a composting worm farm with your little one.

GLADLY GREEN

You enjoy the challenge of reducing waste and delight in every small step you take toward living a more sustainable life. You even schlep empty aluminum cans from the office holiday party to the recycling bin simply because it is too painful to see them in the trash.

OVERWHELMED GREEN

You really would like to make more green choices but feel inundated by the options and utterly unable to live up to your environmental ideals. Limiting your family's impact on the planet is a goal you'd like to achieve—and even feel a bit guilty about—but it may feel impossible in the midst of preparing for baby.

JADED GREEN

While you think it's nice that some people really would like to save the world, it all seems very, well . . . *difficult*. You may be grumbling to yourself, "Whole rainforests are being leveled, what's the point of *me* trying to stop global warming?" Your life is stressful and demanding—the thought of adding more responsibility or complexity to your schedule is too much to bear, especially with a baby on the way.

DEFIANTLY UNGREEN

You don't believe in global warming and drive a Hummer limousine on your five-hundred-mile daily commute. Your children wear nothing but PVC jumpsuits.

The Three Aspirations of *The Eco-nomical Baby Guide:* Save Time, Money, and the Planet

A new baby immediately shakes up old routines and patterns. Even the most conscientious parents might find themselves throwing extra loads of laundry into the wash and cranking up the heat during the winter. When a newborn enters the home, the average family spends 25 percent more on electricity and 13 percent more on natural gas. They'll buy new furniture, toys, and clothes that the little one will outgrow in just a few months. If your child wears disposable diapers, you'll toss out an extra ton of garbage and spend more than $600 in his or her first year alone. All this extra water, heat, trash, and baby gear may start feeling like a necessary component to parenthood. *The Eco-nomical Baby Guide* will show you that you can save time and money while welcoming baby to a greener world.

SAVE TIME

We'll be honest: Oftentimes, going green on a budget does create some extra work. Preparing food from scratch, hanging laundry on the clothesline, and scouring consignment shops for that perfect secondhand high chair do take effort. Hectic schedules may require a few shortcuts as you strive to save the planet. The good news is, some economical activities do shave a few minutes off the clock.

❦ Spare yourself several prebaby shopping trips by finding out exactly what you need—and what you *don't* need—allowing you to cross several items off your list before you even leave the house.

❦ Get practical, up-to-date information on green options for feeding, clothing, diapering, and outfitting your little one, saving you hours of research.

❦ Access a comprehensive list of cost-effective, eco-friendly companies and products instead of wasting time hunting down the best deals on green gear.

❧ Uncover the secrets of easy cloth diapering methods that require no more than ten minutes of hands-on work a week—faster than it takes to run to the store for a pack of Huggies.

SAVE MONEY

Other eco-baby books are enough to make any new parent paranoid about the toxins lurking in everything from applesauce to toy zebras. As a result, you feel pressured to buy all new, organic baby gear. We take a more down-to-earth approach, revealing simple ways to save thousands of dollars on baby's first year. You can pass on the free-trade rattle and organic hair bows!

❧ Instead of shelling out $6,665[1] preparing for baby, find out how to do it for just hundreds.

❧ Learn insider tricks for finding safe, quality used gear for up to 90 percent off retail prices.

❧ Save as much as $1,900 over disposables by embracing our easy cloth-diapering methods. Plan on having two kids? Cloth diapering could save you $4,950![2]

❧ Discover simple techniques for making your own baby food, which can save you a third of what the average family spends on cans of formula and jars of baby food.

❧ Find resources and inspiration for making some of your own baby supplies from recycled or otherwise sustainable materials.

---

[1] Denise and Alan Fields, for their book *Baby Bargains*, surveyed one thousand parents to figure out the average amount parents spend on baby gear in the first year.

[2] In chapter 5 we figure the most expensive disposable diapers (gDiapers) will cost $2,100 per child. Our cheapest cloth diapering option will cost parents $200 for the first baby and just $50 for the second.

SAVE THE PLANET

Mountains of plastic toys, a ton of diapers in a landfill, and pounds of carbon floating up into space—is this the legacy we want to leave our children? Why does modern parenthood seem to involve so much *stuff*? The *Eco-nomical Baby Guide* helps you figure out exactly what you need—and precisely what you *don't* need—to bring up a happy bouncing boy or girl. Thanks in part to our efforts in these early years, our kids will grow up to care about the world they live in.

❄ Keep up to one ton of garbage out of a landfill just by adopting different diapering options.

❄ Learn to understand eco-slang and ensure that products are true to their green claims.

❄ Avoid the average 25 percent increase in energy consumption that baby brings by using simple conservation strategies.

❄ Discover eco-friendly, economical ways to feed baby, from buying local to finding good prices on organic food.

Although you'll find plenty of ways to raise a green baby for less, there are two ingredients that have been purposely omitted from the book: judgment and guilt. Early parenting is hard enough without the pressures of unreachable ideals. The most important lesson we learned in raising our babies is to educate ourselves and then trust our instincts. After all, there is no such thing as a perfect parent or a perfect environmentalist. But as we always say, it's about "progress, not perfection."

Lest you think that we hold ourselves up as model "Earth Mothers," we'll confess to our own eco-failings throughout the book. Did we buy all organic baby gear so our babies would be exposed to as few toxins as possible? No. Did we hang every load of laundry up to dry, warm bottles of expressed breast milk in solar cookers, grow all of our own produce to puree into baby food? No, no, and no! But that doesn't mean we didn't try to find ways to help out the planet while doing the best for our babies—without going broke in the process.

Rather than bogging you down with guilt, *The Eco-nomical Baby Guide* provides a wide range of choices to accommodate your family and your newest addition. It has been written with your environmental goals, busy schedule, and tight baby budget in mind. The time and money you save on stuff can be invested in making memories with your little one. Thanks to your efforts as an eco-conscious parent, your baby will grow up in a greener world—with a bit of green to spare.

The Green Confessional: Sins against Nature

"Forgive me, Mother Earth, for I have sinned. I shower longer than strictly necessary. I buy expensive coffee, and I don't always make sure that it's fair trade—and sometimes I even drink it out of a nonrecyclable paper cup. And though I may brag about never owning a car, the truth is, I have a deep-seated fear of getting behind the wheel."

REBECCA

"Have mercy on my prepackaged food purchases! We toss the boxes and cartons into the recycling bin, but it can't assuage my guilt. I drive twenty minutes each way to work on a daily basis and feel guilty despite my fuel-efficient vehicle. Worst of all, my baby wears a disposable diaper at night because of his devilishly immense bladder capacity."

JOY

CHAPTER

2

Necessities and Niceties:
**What Does Baby
Really Need?**

You stagger bleary-eyed through mega baby stores, a five-page list of "nursery necessities" crumpled in your hands. A couple months and thousands of dollars later, you're wading through piles of shiny, colorful plastic doodads you barely used during your child's infancy. Wasn't all this stuff supposed to make life with a newborn *easier*?

Even green families can get sucked into the consumer vortex when expecting a child. You may be tempted to clutter the nursery with thousands of dollars of nontoxic, eco-friendly "must-haves." Or perhaps you worry about toxins and the environment and wonder how you can even afford organic onesies and free-trade teethers. But before stocking up, step back. Remember that the easiest way to be eco-friendly *is to simply avoid purchasing so many of the "must-have" gadgets and devices on the market.* It's the oldest environmental tip in the book: reduce. This chapter will offer clever suggestions for reducing the amount of clothes, toys, gadgets, and gizmos threatening to turn your living room into a jungle gym. And the best part is, you'll find how going green can save you as much as 85 percent of what the average American spends on baby gear.

Nursery Necessities

If you ask a big-box store for its recommended registry, you'll be handed a list packed with hundreds of items you've never heard of or can't imagine needing, from a peekaboo cover to toilet locks. Don't panic—you don't need to get everything before baby arrives. All you need to be prepared for baby's arrival is listed below.

❁ A place for baby to sleep

❁ A way to feed baby

❁ A way to diaper baby

❁ A way to keep baby warm

❁ A way to care for baby's health and safety

We'll go through each category so you can decide if you really need to buy an item or if you already have something that will serve your purpose. Once you do choose to buy something, you'll have to decide whether to get it used (always a green choice) or new.

A PLACE FOR BABY TO SLEEP

If you plan to have baby sleep in bed with you, you're all set! If you don't want to co-sleep, you'll need to buy a crib or some sort of bassinet. After spending time with your newborn, you'll eventually figure out a sleeping arrangement that works for the whole family.

Green Ideas

👣 **Skip the crib.** Some people avoid using a crib or bassinet altogether by opting to sleep in a "family bed" with their little ones, especially at first when the need for nighttime nursing is so great.

👣 **Don't get a bassinet.** A baby can sleep in a crib right from the beginning. While a bassinet can be convenient, it's not necessary.

❦ **Try a Moses basket if you do want a bassinet.** This is just what it sounds like—a basket designed for small babies (less than fifteen pounds) to sleep in. Its fiber construction is much friendlier to the environment than plastic, and it's easily transportable around the house. Depending on the size of baby, you might be able to use it for quite some time before your child needs a crib. A Moses basket could also eliminate the need for other baby resting places such as a swing, bouncer seat, or play gym. Later it can be used to store toys.

❦ **Use a Pack-N-Play as a crib,** which can double as a bassinet and diaper-changing station. If you are going to buy a travel crib, do you need a regular crib as well?

❦ **Be wary of the cribs that convert to toddler beds.** Some companies require you to purchase other products, so research this carefully. Furthermore, if you intend to have more than one child, the more logical option is to purchase a standard crib and move your first child into a regular bed when he or she's old enough.

Gear Up for a Grand: How We Did It

While we both took slightly different approaches to gearing up for our new babies, neither of us spent much more than $1,000 on baby gear—including diaper and food costs—in our babies' first year. Compare that to the national average of almost $7,000!

How did we do it? Rebecca chose the minimalist approach. She heard great things about swings, bouncy seats, and play gyms, all of which promised to keep the baby amused for twenty-minute stretches of time. And she resisted. Cluttering her tiny house with something that her daughter would grow out of in just three months wasn't worth it to her. Three months later, she found she had survived without any of those glorified baby resting spots.

Joy's son Roscoe's nursery featured a glider rocker, play gym, *and* an Exersaucer. She'd spent many months of her pregnancy trolling around Craigslist for used baby bargains. One day she answered an ad from a woman who wanted to get rid of her baby equipment. The woman stuffed Joy's car with all the baby gadgets she could dream of—all for free! So while she didn't exactly take the ascetic route, she stayed true to her green ideals by finding used gear and passing it on when she was through with it.

A WAY TO FEED BABY

If you plan to breastfeed and will be home with baby for a few months, you have just about everything you'll need. Working moms will most likely want a pump, a few bottles, and the accompanying equipment.

Green Ideas for Nursing Mothers

❦ **Check your insurance policy before stocking up on nursing supplies.** Some hospitals and birthing centers provide the basics: nursing pads, a pump, and a tube of lanolin to help with sensitive nipples in those early weeks. Rebecca scored a free manual breast pump and some storage bottles at the hospital, so she was glad she hadn't purchased one.

❦ **Wait on nursing bras.** Your bra size can fluctuate for a while right before and after giving birth. You could also use regular bras or sports bras and simply pull them up or down as needed.

❦ **Try reusable breast pads.** Some nursing mothers need pads only in the first few weeks, when their milk first comes in, and others rely on them for as long as they nurse. Disposable pads have several drawbacks—they are expensive in the long run and create waste on a daily basis. Reusable pads are comfortable and easy to use. (We recommend LANAcare wool pads.)

❦ **Don't rule out used breast pumps.** Craigslist and consignment shops sell breast pumps for quite a bit cheaper than new. You can also rent electric pumps from the hospital. If you opt to buy used, most pump manufacturers recommend that you buy new tubing and attachments (available in many mainstream retail stores) for sanitary purposes.

Green Ideas for Bottle-feeding Families

❦ **If you are planning on feeding your baby formula or expressed breast milk, you'll need at least one bottle to start out**. If baby is in daycare full time, you might not need to provide bottles since many facilities have them available, but you may want a few extra on hand just in case. Remember that some babies are very picky about which ones they like so it's best to forgo the starter kits and buy them individually at first.

❦ **Choose glass instead of plastic bottles**—glass is making a comeback as more parents become concerned about toxins leaching from plastic bottles. They also have a much longer lifespan than plastic bottles, making them an eco-friendly choice.

❦ **Don't buy unnecessary sterilization equipment.** If you have a dishwasher, no further sterilization equipment for bottles will be necessary. You could boil bottles in an open pan of boiling water to sterilize, but if you plan to do this frequently, it would be worth it to buy a microwave or electric sterilizer—these would use less energy and water than the old-fashioned method. Many parents simply wash bottles normally instead of using sterilizing equipment, though.

A WAY TO DIAPER BABY

Don't panic if you haven't figured out a diapering system before baby is born, although it doesn't hurt to think of the options. One pack of newborn-size disposables or a dozen cloth diapers is all you really need to get through the first week. This section will provide you with a few "greener ideas" for reducing waste when gearing up. (For more information on choosing a diapering system, turn to chapter 5.)

Green Ideas

❦ **Do without!** Is it possible to avoid using diapers altogether? Maybe. Ambitious green parents make do without buying any diapers at all by practicing infant potty training (see chapter 5 for more details).

❦ **Consider cloth.** Using cloth isn't as difficult as it once was—no more pins or plastic pants! If you don't want to launder diapers yourself, there is the option of a diaper service. Diaper services bring a fresh stack of diapers to your door each week, whisking away the dirty ones so you don't have to wash them.

❦ **Try "greener" disposables.** Not all disposable diapers are alike—some can even be flushed down the toilet. Seventh Generation and Whole Foods 365 brand both make a chlorine-free disposable. Hybrid diapers such as gDiapers have a flushable (or compostable) insert inside a cloth cover.

❦ **Skip the changing table.** You can create more room in your home and less waste in the world by being creative with what is available to you. Use the top of baby's dresser as a changing table or use furniture surfaces in other parts of the house. As you will quickly find out, baby can be changed anywhere. Many parents feel more comfortable changing their babies on the floor, so you might choose to set up your diapering station there right from the start.

❦ **Have your diaper pail do double-duty.** You don't need a white, plastic diaper pail. You can use any 5-gallon receptacle, such as a bucket with a lid or a standard lidded trash can. The advantage of this is that once your diapering days are over, your diaper pail will enjoy a second life as a garbage bin.

❦ **Look for diapers (even disposables) on Craigslist or eBay.** If you are planning on using disposables, you can sometimes snag parents' extras by looking online. Used cloth diapers and diaper covers can be a great value and are easily sanitized.

 Eco-nomical Tip

Switching to cloth diapers will save you between $1,000 and $5,000, depending on how many children you have. Plus, for every child you swaddle in cloth, you'll be keeping a ton of waste out of the landfill.

A WAY TO KEEP BABY WARM

For the first week, you can swaddle baby in one of the millions of blankets you're likely to receive as gifts. Parents often get so caught up in the variety of cute clothing available to them that they forget just how briefly their child will be wearing it. First of all, your baby would be adorable in any fashion, color, or cut, and second, you will most likely be receiving heaps of baby clothes from friends and family. Cutting back on clothes means being able to use less storage space, getting some good wear out of items that baby will have for a few months, and having more room in your home.

It usually does not pay off to stock up on baby clothes too far in advance. Each of us had several adorable outfits given to our babies that they were *never* able to wear. Rebecca's long and skinny baby never fit in some boxier styles. And Joy's son Roscoe grew so quickly that he skipped past his newborn sizes and was wearing three-month clothes within the first few weeks. It's also hard to predict how quickly baby will grow; just because your baby is six months old in the summer doesn't mean he or she will necessarily fit in the six-month size at that point.

Green Ideas

❧ **Wait before stocking up on clothing** to avoid wasting time and money (not to mention several yards of cotton).

❧ **Be creative with storage furniture.** Do you really need a dresser? Do you have a closet with shelves that would work just as well? Baby clothes take up very little space and can be stored in creative ways. Can you empty out a few drawers in your own bureau? Do you have another piece of furniture that you could use for stowing baby clothes?

❧ **Think about pieces of furniture that will be multiuse.** Can the dresser double as a changing table? Can bookshelves from another room be moved into the nursery to hold baby's possessions?

A WAY TO CARE FOR BABY'S HEALTH AND SAFETY: CAR SEATS

Unfortunately, car seats are made out of several pounds of plastic that must be thrown away after about five years (which is when they "expire"). Car seats are also not a purchase many people feel comfortable getting used—but it is possible to get a safe used seat if you follow the correct guidelines (see chapter 3).

There are many factors to consider when purchasing car seats for different phases of baby's life. Look in a consumer guide such as *Baby Bargains* or *The Consumer Reports Best Baby Products* for specific safety and convenience features of different brands and styles.

The laws concerning car seats vary by state, but in general it is advised that babies and children ride in car seats from birth to around age eight—or when they are at least 4'9" (57 inches). Visit www.aap.org or www.nhtsa.dot.gov to figure out what car seats will work for the various phases in a child's life.

Green Ideas

❧ **Get an all-in-one seat.** These are relatively new on the market, and there aren't many models available, but if you find one you are happy with, this would work from birth until baby doesn't need a car seat any more. If you have multiple cars, you could get one for each car, and you would end up with just two seats for all baby's car seat needs. (Compare this with the five or more seats you would need if you decided on the infant seat, convertible, then booster combination for each car.) If you have subsequent children, these seats will work just as well for them, too, no matter how the children are spaced.

❧ **Skip the infant seat.** Although many parents like the convenience of the infant seat, it is not necessary. You can just use convertible car seats or all-in-ones.

❧ **If you do have an infant seat, do not buy a second base for a second car.** The seats can be belted into vehicles much more quickly than other types of car seats. The base is a convenience feature, not a safety feature.

❧ **If you have multiple cars, think of possible solutions to avoid buying a car seat for each car.** One option is to designate one car the "car seat car." We do not recommend taking convertible or all-in-ones in and out of cars on a daily basis—correct installation is important, and it's better to keep them safely installed at all times, even if it means buying extra car seats.

❧ **Once you have decided on what you want for the new baby (an infant seat, convertible seat, or an all-in-one), don't buy the next seat until you need it!** You could save yourself unnecessary purchases. For example, if you have an infant seat and baby fits in it up until the first year, you don't need a convertible seat at all—you can go directly to a forward-facing harness booster. This option did not work for either of us. Joy's baby outgrew the infant seat before a year and needed a convertible seat. Rebecca's baby didn't weigh twenty pounds at a year, but outgrew the height limit of the infant seat, so she needed a convertible seat to keep her baby backward-facing for a few more months. There are advantages to having an infant car seat, but both of us wondered if we should have simply started with the convertible seat (or an all-in-one seat) and saved a purchase.

❧ **Ask around to see if anyone would like to borrow your seat** once your baby has outgrown it if you have taken care of it and haven't been in an accident. This is an especially viable option for the infant seat, which is usually used for a year or less. You could save someone else a purchase and several pounds of plastic from a landfill. If you time it right, you can get it back before you have a second child.

❧ **Look at how much the car seats you're considering weigh.** Some convertible car seats weigh up to twenty-three pounds and others weigh just eleven. The lighter seats use fewer materials and are therefore better for the environment.

A WAY TO CARE FOR BABY'S HEALTH AND SAFETY: OTHER SAFETY ITEMS

You can use your own thermometer (tucked into baby's armpit) and nail file instead of buying specially advertised baby versions. Also, many hospitals give out ball syringes for clearing baby's nose. The other option is to register for an infant health kit at any mainstream store, or ask for the individual pieces that you think you'll most need. Most kits come with a thermometer, infant nail clippers, and a ball syringe.

Baby Gear You Don't Need

"I used the Baby Bargains book to guide me on this, and there were very few things I got that I didn't use. Most of what I did get was either a hand-me-down, garage sale or Craigslist find, or a gift. I plan on handing down to friends and family, too, so it will all get reused. We saved tons of money this way and didn't create more waste, which was important to us."

RONICA SKARPHOL BROWNSON, State College, Pennsylvania

"The one that gets me is posh diaper bags. It's, like, people don't realize that the backpack under their bed will work just as well if not better. It might not have gone with my fashionable ensembles (ha!), but it didn't scream Gullible Consumer, either."

ANONYMOUS

"Slings are fab—no need for a huge pushchair, and you get to keep your babe close to you all the time (so then you don't need loads of covers and blankets, because your baby is kept at a constant temperature close to you)."

RACHELLE STRAUSS, UK, of littlegreenblog.com and myzerowaste.com

"Those 'bedding sets' they advertise that are so cute are a huge waste of money. Except for the diaper stacker and the crib sheet, we never used any of it, and of course you can buy crib sheets separately, and I could just as easily have kept the diapers in the top drawer of the dresser."

LARISA MOORE, Seattle, Washington

Greening Your Baby Shower

You're into cloth diapers, glass bottles, and burlap burp rags. Your dear friend has offered to throw you a baby shower—yahoo! The problem? She's more of the disposable diaper and throwaway sippy cup persuasion. Are you going to be stuck with a pile of gifts that you don't want and don't need?

It can be hard to accept gifts that don't meet your criteria for the perfect green nursery, but remember that your friends are celebrating with the best of intentions. They probably don't understand your desire for eco-baby gear . . . or they may not even be aware such a thing exists! There are a few things you can do:

Express yourself . . . when asked. While it's rude to solicit gifts of any kind, some may ask you what you want or need. This is the time to make your wishes clear.

Ask for less, receive more. If you are selective in your gift registry or find other suggestions for gifts, you might not end up with twenty-seven pairs of baby booties and one tube of diaper paste when all the presents are unwrapped. Registering for less gives you a higher likelihood of getting everything you want. It also eliminates the need to trek back to stores for returns when you are extremely pregnant or toting your new baby.

Register for green gear. Well-intentioned friends and family often purchase baby items that you might not necessarily want for your child: crates of disposable diapers, boxes of plastic toys, and endless newborn outfits that your child will wear for less than a week. So how can you guide gift-givers toward your green choices? Check to see if any local, eco-friendly baby boutiques have registries. If you're nowhere near such a store, the Internet provides several options.

Consider a diaper shower. This is a fabulous idea to help you deal with the front-end expense of buying cloth diapers or gDiapers. Consider registering at a store or an online diaper outlet that carries alternative diapers and accessories, which can cost quite a bit depending on the brands and styles you want. When pressed for gift ideas, the host can even encourage guests to pay for some months of a diaper service.

❦ **Delay the gratification.** Asking for gift cards or certificates to consignment shops can help you grapple with later costs in baby's life. Think about asking for housecleaning or meal delivery in those first few weeks of parenthood. In short, think outside the gift registry box.

❦ **Leave the "shower" out of "baby shower."** It's possible to have a party with friends, family, and games without involving gifts. Let everyone know you want only their presence and their good wishes. Participants can even write out hopes or blessings for the new addition that the host can make into a keepsake book. Or circumvent the baby shower ritual altogether and involve friends and family in a picnic, hike, or other decidedly "non-showery" celebration.

❦ **Take it back!** Perhaps the path of least resistance . . . simply accept not-so-green gifts in the spirit that they are given. And then return what you don't want—or donate it to charity.

Tips for Hosting an Eco-nomical Baby Shower

❧ **Ditch the disposable decor.** Does the celebration of a new baby really need to involve baby cutouts of rattles and bottles? Do you need to festoon the ceiling with pink and blue streamers? A few cut flowers from the yard (or the florist) can brighten a room just as well.

❧ **Dine on real dishes.** Pick up a set of dishes at a thrift shop and use them exclusively for birthday parties, showers, and family gatherings. Don't want to wash dishes after the party? Choose paper plates made from recycled materials. Chinet's paper plates are made from 100 percent recycled materials and can be composted once the party's over.

❧ **Try a "secondhand" baby shower.** If almost everyone you know has had babies in the last few years, a secondhand shower can be an entertaining way to pass treasured belongings from one family to another. Of course, this idea might not fly with many expecting parents or hosts—but it just might be right up a green family's alley.

How I Threw an Eco Baby Shower (by Rebecca)

When my sister-in-law announced her pregnancy, the first thing that popped into my head was not, "All right, a new cousin for Audrey!" but, "All right, I can throw a green baby shower!" Because someone had already put on a huge extravaganza in Amanda's hometown, I knew she didn't need to be showered with even more high chairs, baby clothes, and silver rattles.

That's when I decided to host a book baby shower. The theme was perfect, considering that Amanda and I both belonged to the same book club. I knew she loved to read and wanted to pass that love onto her child. In my invitations, which I made look like little books—complete with a ribbon bookmark—I asked everyone to bring a copy (new or used) of a favorite childhood book.

I held the shower in my own house, made the food myself, and served everything on real dishes. Opening the books was the highlight of the party, as everyone reminisced about their childhood favorites. We even entertained ourselves with some dramatic readings of *Goodnight Moon* and *The Very Hungry Caterpillar*.

How are book baby showers greener than other showers? Unlike most baby gear, books entertain a child for years. People often hang on to their childhood favorites well into adulthood and pass them on to their own children. They do more to enhance a child's learning than any plastic, battery-operated toy, they're reasonably priced, and they're even biodegradable!

Niceties

If you have the necessities, you're all set for baby's arrival. Everything else can be filed away in the "niceties" category—things that make life easier for you or more comfortable for the little one.

Common Niceties

🌷 Rocking chair or glider

🌷 Swing or bouncer

🌷 Slings, backpacks, or front packs

🌷 Travel crib

🌷 Nursery decorations

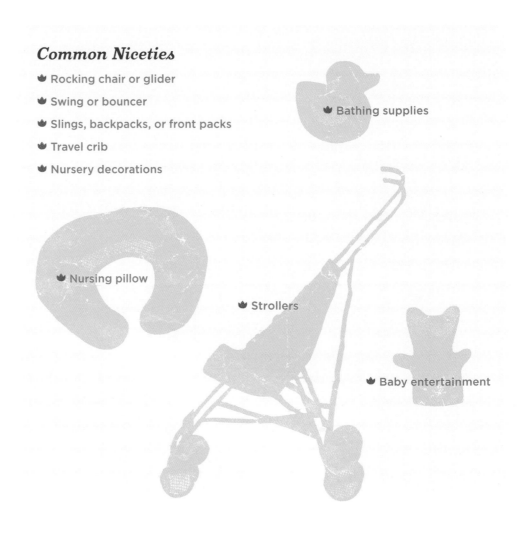

🌷 Bathing supplies

🌷 Nursing pillow

🌷 Strollers

🌷 Baby entertainment

GREEN IDEAS FOR NICETIES

❦ **Wait.** Don't buy everything before baby arrives—you might get what you need as gifts, and you won't need them for quite a while. Try baby contraptions *after* baby is born so that you can decide whether to buy something. Some babies lie contentedly in a bouncer and others do not. Ditto on slings, swings, and every other gizmo you can think of.

❦ **Use what you have.** Dancing and jiggling can replace the soothing movements of a rocker. A fan makes a great white-noise machine. Dishpans, storage tubs, and the kitchen sink all function as miniature bathtubs. Babies don't necessarily need special chairs, swings, or other resting spots, especially in the first few months when they will lie contentedly on a blanket on the floor without rolling away.

❦ **Keep it simple.** In America we have become obsessed with educational gizmos designed to help our children get a head start on their peers. Plastic contraptions that teach the alphabet, colors, and numbers are not going to make any child a genius. In fact, most of history's geniuses played with wooden blocks, bugs, and their own toes. Don't get sucked into purchasing loads of developmental toys that you then trip over on the living room floor.

❦ **Consider the lifespan of the contraption.** A play gym entertains babies for just a few months before they roll over and move on.

❦ **Don't let a bargain keep you from buying quality.** Joy's cheap glider didn't seem like such a good deal when her back was aching as she tried rocking a screaming baby to sleep at three in the morning.

❦ **Think simple and gender neutral.** Instead of painting the nursery floor to ceiling and outfitting each corner with color-coordinated doodads, keep it simple. Use accents to decorate the nursery that will interest your child as he or she grows older. Less decorating frenzies mean less stress, less waste, and less expense.

❦ **Consider your lifestyle.** How often do you think you'd use something? What is the minimum that would fulfill your requirements? Do you want to invest in something with all the bells and whistles if you'll use it just a few times a month?

Rebecca and Joy's Niceties

So did we, two self-described green mothers, indulge in any niceties? Yes! No one is ever going to agree on what is a "must-have" and what is a complete waste of money. But here are the niceties we ended up with—for better or for worse.

"I skipped the glider and the swing or bouncer—and I didn't miss them one bit. I couldn't have lived without a stroller, though! While my $5 handmade sling saved my sanity in those first few months, the stroller got almost constant use for three years. Because I don't have a car and do all my errands by foot, I preferred the stroller to other baby-carrying devices, especially as my daughter got heavier."

REBECCA

"We vowed not to indulge in a baby bath or a sling, sure that our child could easily slip into a sink full of bubbles and be calmed in our arms. Later we ended up buying a bath to save water (and our backs), and friends gave us a Maya Wrap sling and a Kangaroo Korner sling. The slings were incredibly effective at calming our colicky son—for us they became our two most important pieces of gear after just a few days."

JOY

Avoiding Desperation Purchases

There is a happy medium between buying every possible bit of gear before baby is born and waiting to get it all after he or she arrives. Every obstacle you encounter in the early months of caring for a newborn can seem like a dire emergency as your clumsy mind struggles with sleep deprivation, hormones, and baby bliss. In our first weeks as moms, we both made "desperation purchases" as we attempted to solve the problem of sheer exhaustion with a product. In both cases, the item proved totally useless.

Every new parent is certainly allowed a few totally irrational purchases, but since they aren't generally helpful to you, your baby, *or* the environment, have a plan in place so that you can limit those frantic shopping trips. Joy ended up pacing through Target with her cell phone, giddy with fatigue as her sister tried to talk her down from buying every swing on the market. To avoid a similar fate, don't venture out by yourself if you need something in those early days. Have friends or family get you the product, help you set it up, and keep the receipt on hand so that they can run it back to the store for you if it doesn't work out.

Holding Back the Flood of Baby Gear: Rebecca's Experience

First of all, I have to admit that I'm the kind of person who thinks it's a good idea to put a baby in a drawer instead of a crib. While for some people the image of a baby snuggled in a drawer harkens back to simpler times—or hard times—for me it smacks of ingenuity. When the baby has outgrown the makeshift bassinet, the drawer goes right back in the dresser to store her socks. How clever! While we ended up with a real crib instead of a drawer, I still had a strong desire to stop the flood of baby gear from making its way into our house. The thought of a living room piled to the ceiling with colorful, blinking plastic noisemakers was enough to send waves of panic through me.

Eco-nomical Tip

Save several hundred dollars and a small corner of landfill space just by choosing to buy less baby equipment.

Baby Bargains (2007) by Denise and Alan Fields includes the chart below, citing the amount of money the average American will spend on baby gear in the baby's first year.[3] The second column shows the amount you can spend using their book as a guide. Always up for a tightwad challenge, I faithfully recorded every penny I spent on the baby in her first year. As you can see, I saved about 85 percent of what the average American spends and 75 percent of what the *Baby Bargains* readers spend.

Big disclaimer: We received a lot of stuff for free, thanks to the generosity of friends and family. We didn't pay for a crib, Moses basket, stroller, baby carrier, or car seat. The crib was a hand-me-down, but everything else totaled more than $400. We also received countless outfits, toys, and blankets as gifts. This skews my final numbers quite a bit. If you have to fund all of your baby gear yourself, don't despair—you can still score much of your baby gear for free, as we discuss in chapter 3. Remember that a big advantage of not getting so many gifts is that you can buy everything according to your own tastes. I know I dressed my baby in many outfits I never would have picked out myself.

Comparing Costs:
How Does Minimizing Save Me Money?

ITEM	AVERAGE	BUDGET	OURS
Crib, mattress, dresser, rocker	$1600	$1300	$180
Maternity and nursing clothes	$1260	$540	$277
Baby food/formula	$950	$350	$92.17
Diapers	$630	$300	$160.09
Baby clothes	$525	$335	$88.50
Nursery items, high chairs, toys	$425	$225	$83
Stroller, car seat, carrier	$425	$334	$0
Bedding and decor	$315	$154	$65
Miscellaneous	$525	$500	$60
Total	**$6,665**	**$4,038**	**$1,005.76**

[3] *Baby Bargains* surveyed more than one thousand parents to arrive at these figures.

Rebecca's Itemized Costs, Broken Down

CRIB, MATTRESS, DRESSER ROCKER	$180
crib bumper	$10
dresser	$170

MATERNITY AND NURSING CLOTHES	$277
breast pads	$21
nursing camisole	$17
milk bags	$10
various other garments	$229

BABY FOOD/FORMULA	$92.17
organic formula	$56
solid foods	$32.42
bottle	$3.75

DIAPERS	$160.09
36 prefold diapers	$50
6 Proraps covers (used but appear new)	$8.50
disposables and travel wipes	$35
washing/drying diapers (estimated cost)	$66.59[4]

BABY CLOTHES	$88.50
assortment of baby clothes purchased while pregnant	$40
dress for wedding	$5.50
overalls	$2
pajamas	$2
5 onesies	$3
4 shirts, overalls, onesie, sweater	$10
sweater	$8
Halloween pumpkin costume	$2.50
hoodie	$5
velvet dress, onesie, jeans	$10.50

NURSERY ITEMS, HIGH CHAIRS, TOYS	$83
high chair	$50
changing pad	$20
diaper pail	$28
blanket and toy	$16
pacifier	$3

STROLLER, CAR SEAT, CARRIER	$0
all hand-me-downs or gifts	$0

BEDDING AND DECOR	$65
rug	$35
paint supplies	$20
blanket	$10

Miscellaneous

My budget is just an example. You could take a look at ten parents' "must have" lists and every one would contain something you never wanted or your baby refused to use—every parent is different, and each baby has his or her own preferences. Obviously parents will want to balance their desire to save money and help the environment with their own taste and quirks.

....

[4] See chapter 6 to figure out how much washing and drying will cost for you. I washed in cold water in a front-loading machine, which cost me $19.79/year. I also tumble dried all those diaper loads, which set me back $46.80.

WE COULD HAVE SAVED EVEN MORE MONEY

If spending the absolute minimum had been our goal, we could have spent much less. Here are a few examples, with our reasoning behind choosing a more expensive option:

❀ **We spent $28 on a stainless-steel push-pedal garbage can** to use as a diaper pail when a plastic 5-gallon bucket with a lid from the hardware store costs just $5. We opted for the fancy trash can for aesthetic and environmental reasons: once we no longer need a diaper pail, we'll wash it out and use it as a regular trash can.

❀ **We probably could have found a free dresser and saved $170.** Especially considering that our $170 afforded us a shoddy dresser that we needed to replace just a few years later.

❀ **I am just too vain to wear my husband's jeans and bulky sweaters** for the sake of anticonsumerism and the environment, but it would have saved me $277 in maternity clothes.

Toy Tip

Tiffany, a green mom of four, rotates her children's playthings by storing some of them in the garage every few months. When she pulls them out every so often her children feel as though they have new toys to play with, helping her minimize the toys in her living space and keep things fresh for her kids.

The Top Ten Most Fun Household Objects for Baby

Our informal poll of families from around the country left us with the top ten favorite household items babies sometimes love more than their "real" toys. See if this list works for your little one.

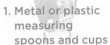

3. Tupperware containers and lids

2. Phones, remotes, and keys

1. Metal or plastic measuring spoons and cups

7. Plastic cups and plates

5. Rubber spatulas and wooden spoons

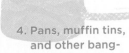

4. Pans, muffin tins, and other bang-able items

6. Refrigerator magnets

8. The laundry basket

9. Cardboard boxes

10. Wrapping paper

WE COULD HAVE MADE SOME GREENER CHOICES

In our desire to be green we focused mainly on minimizing, with the idea that it's better for the planet to forgo a bouncy seat altogether than to buy one. Looking back at my purchases, I see a few ways I could have been eco-friendlier:

❧ **We could have bought a used car seat.** We opted for new. There are so many factors to consider when purchasing a car seat that once we'd decided on the make and model we wanted, we didn't want to spend the energy looking for it used.

❧ **We could have bought cloth diapers made from hemp or unbleached organic cotton.** I chose standard bleached prefolds with the idea that if they got stained, I could bleach them again. Not the greenest idea I ever had. At the time I did not think much about the way the diapers were produced, and I opted to buy new because I wanted to be sure I was getting "diaper service quality" diapers.

❧ **We could have made more of an effort to travel with cloth diapers.** It just seemed easier to bring disposables for plane travel so we wouldn't have to worry about washing diapers at someone else's house or at a hotel.

❧ **We could have line-dried our diapers.** This would have saved almost $50 and almost 40 pounds of carbon dioxide.

❧ **We could have used "greener" paint for the nursery.** At the time I didn't consider the environmental impact of standard paints.

Trust Your Instincts!

No amount of gear, advice, or experience will totally prepare you for raising a tiny baby, but believe it or not, you can handle it! Trust your own abilities and remember that parents have been doing this job for thousands of years. The most important resources you will need are instincts, flexibility, and a sense of humor—all of which are great for your newest family member and the environment.

Resources

Check out these books to read reviews of much of the mainstream baby gear on the market:

⚙ *Baby Bargains* by Denise and Alan Fields

⚙ *Consumer Reports Best Baby Products*

⚙ *Itsabelly's Guide to Going Green with Baby* by Jennifer Lo Prete and Melissa Moog

The sites below all offer online registries and gift shopping for your baby's adoring public.

⚙ **Our Green House** (www.ourgreenhouse.com) This site specializes in green items for your home and your baby.

⚙ A unique type of registry, **My Gift List** (www.mygiftlist.com) allows you to register for any product from any store. You can create one registry that includes several products from different online shops. It's quick, easy, and allows you to pick an eclectic assortment.

⚙ **Momma's Baby** (www.mommasbaby.com) offers a whole range of baby products such as slings, Moses baskets, and cloth diapers in addition to lotions, personal care items, and other treats for mothers-to-be. The online registry is extremely user friendly.

⚙ For family members who feel more comfortable going to the store and seeing what they're buying than purchasing something online, **Babies R Us** (www.babiesrus.com) is a good option. Their green product lines are expanding every year, but they don't have much selection for cloth diapers.

3

Save Cash and Save the Planet: **Buy Used Gear**

Bamboo blankets, free-trade rattles, organic booties—is this what it takes to raise a green baby? You may be heartened to know that the best way to limit environmental impact does not involve spending a fortune on all things eco—in fact, buying secondhand gear could end up saving you thousands of dollars.

The "hand-me-down" approach to acquiring baby paraphernalia may seem rather old school, but in many ways getting used gear is a better environmental option than purchasing a newly manufactured eco-healthy item. You'll keep packaging materials out of your house, save as much as 90 percent over retail prices, and keep one more piece of baby equipment from a landfill. Plus, you'll help eliminate the environmental cost of manufacturing and shipping.

The economic factor alone is tremendous motivation to consider secondhand goods. The average family spends $6,665 on their baby *just in the first year*—most of which goes to purchase brand-new products that are used for just a few months. The $7.1 billion baby product industry would like you to continue supporting its growing market share, but there are other options. Why not tuck away a bit of your baby budget for the future, find some quality used gear, and save the earth at the same time?

The deals you can find when buying used can be truly astonishing. Purchasing secondhand gear can save 40 to 60 percent or more off of big-ticket purchases such as cribs and strollers and 50 to 90 percent off lower-cost goods like clothes and toys.

As we've scoured ads and thrift stores, we've seen the following bargains:

✿ A $700 Pottery Barn crib for $245

✿ A $90 Graco high chair for $15

✿ $25 to $45 Gap baby clothes for $1 to $7

✿ $10 to $20 baby bath tubs for as low as $5—or free!

Plus, sometimes a bargain can lead to more free loot. Joy lucked out while picking up a brand-new crib mattress advertised on Craigslist. The seller had just decided to clean out the nursery and loaded up Joy's car with bags of clothes, linens, and toys—all for free!

Tips from the Trenches: Green Parents Discuss Gearing Up

"We almost exclusively used inherited or used gear. Baby consignment shops are usually high quality, barely used, and a fraction of the cost. Get involved with a gear sharing co-op of moms or even a group of women that trade and share items around the group."

AMY MCKENNEY, Bellingham, Washington

"One of the biggest elements of our green awareness is to simply reduce what we have or avoid buying new items altogether. For clothes shopping and various household items, thrift stores are our first stop."

LESLEY WOODRUFF, Newberg, Oregon

"One of the advantages of being the last among friends and family to have kids is gleaning lots of advice and baby gear. Over and over, we heard the same two things: 'Less is more' and 'Do you want these barely used clothes and toys?' In spite of the fact that we practically never go shopping at the mall, Samuel looks smashing and has plenty of stimulating, age-appropriate toys."

JENNIFER WALWORTH, Missoula, Montana

Quiz: How Green Art Thou?

1. **IN PLANNING FOR BABY'S ARRIVAL, YOU DECIDE A CRIB IS A NECESSITY. WHAT'S THE GREENEST CRIB OPTION?**

A. A new crib crafted from sustainable wood or bamboo.

B. A used crib passed down from a family member or bought from a garage sale.

C. A bargain-priced new crib purchased at a baby warehouse.

D. A hemp hammock in the corner of the nursery. Throwing caution to the wind, you decide that baby will quickly learn *not* to roll over.

Answer: Forgoing a crib altogether is the best solution for the environment, but that wasn't an option on the quiz, and it may not feasible for your family. **The best answer is B:** Get your hands on a used crib. However, many other guide-books and safety advocates recommend never using a secondhand crib for a child. Is buying a crib made of sustainable materials the only eco-friendly choice? We believe buying used can still be an option for safety-minded families. We'll discuss this later in the chapter so you can make up your own mind.

2. **YOUR LITTLE BAMBINO *NEEDS* AN EXERSAUCER AND MANY OTHER EDUCATIONAL CONTRAPTIONS ON THE MARKET. WHAT'S GREENEST?**

A. Treasure hunting for your used dream nursery on Craigslist.

B. Purchasing the latest store-bought equipment (because you just love the smell of pristine plastic!).

C. Finding eco-friendly alternative products made from cloth, hemp, or other materials.

D. Building an Exersaucer out of recycled tin cans, chewing gum, and scrap lumber.

Answer: A. You may be amazed with your natural ability to soothe your child using what you already have—funny facial gestures and your pinkie finger as a pacifier. If you still want a few gizmos, you can prevent bringing new hunks of plastic into the world by buying them used. Once these items are here, they will have the least impact by being used by as many babies as possible.

What about greener baby goods? Do they even make a bamboo Exersaucer? Maybe not, but if you look around, you may find better alternatives. Check out chapter 4 for eco-friendly suggestions.

3. YOU ARE SEARCHING FOR "GREEN" WAYS TO OUTFIT YOUR CHILD. WHAT DO YOU DO?

A. Use your crafty wisdom to knit and sew handmade garments.

B. Search stores and Internet outlets for clothing woven from organic hemp and cotton.

C. Look for baby fashions at a consignment shop where pre-owned merchandise is sold at great prices.

D. Simplify the little one's wardrobe by outfitting him or her solely in a diaper, layering with a blanket or two in the colder months.

Answer: C. Buying used is easy, cheap, and undeniably green. Bargain-hunting shoppers can find secondhand name-brand clothing for 60 to 95 percent less than it would cost new. The U.S. Department of Agriculture estimates that the average family spends more than $600 on baby clothing in the first year alone, but you could end up saving yourself hundreds by buying quality resale clothing.

Of course, some consumers seek out organic clothes not just because they are good for the Earth, but because they believe they're better for baby.

The Downside of Used Gear

While everyone loves a deal, we all struggle with the "yuck factor." Sometimes finding dried-up baby food on a used item can make you feel downright icky about offering it to your little one, even if the rational part of you knows it can be cleaned. Remember that in a matter of minutes, the most sanitized new toy will be coated in your child's slobber and/or mucus.

Even if you manage to fully outfit the nursery with pre-owned treasures, grandparents and relatives often want to give store-bought presents to baby. You may want to ask them for the new items that you know you want for safety, aesthetic, or functional reasons. Another option is to request gift cards or certificates when asked for ideas. These provide you with the flexibility to carefully select what you need later in baby's life and avoid getting overrun with odds and ends you wouldn't have chosen yourself.

You may consider buying some items new because of safety issues, especially when it comes to car seats and cribs. (Turn to the end of this chapter for more safety information.) The car seat, in particular, may be one purchase for which you decide to go the conventional route. If you have a car or will travel in a car, there's really no getting around buying a car seat, and each one is made out of several pounds of plastic. If you decide to buy new, you can take good care of the car seat and pass it on for family and friends or use it again if you have another child. As long as it hasn't been in an accident and isn't more than five years old, this is considered safe. An average baby usually outgrows the infant seat in under a year. If five babies can use it before it expires, that will save four infant car seats from winding up in a landfill. That's about forty pounds of plastic!

Eco-nomical Tip

Secondhand shopping will save you *at least* 40 percent on baby gear. You'll also cut down on the carbon emitted from producing raw materials, manufacturing the product, packaging it, and shipping it across the country.

The Seven Best Sources for Used Baby Gear

The happy anticipation of expectant parents often fades into financial panic when they start eyeing the baby registry list. Jen Nyborg, green mother of five with nearly a decade of secondhand shopping experience, has always faced her budget challenges creatively. "Having a baby doesn't have to be a huge expense. If you think of shopping for bargains as treasure hunting, it can really be fun," she says. Use the following tips to make your search all the more fruitful.

1. **Friends and Family.** Notify family, friends, and co-workers that you welcome their hand-me-downs. Other parents will often happily unload the baby paraphernalia cluttering their homes or loan it out until their next child arrives. Consider starting a "Got and Want" bulletin board at work where people offer their extras and post their needs.

2. **Freecycle.** If you agree to offer up your unwanted stuff through freecycle.com, you'll get listings from several local people who are unloading their extras—all at no cost. You may be surprised at what some people consider trash and others consider treasure. Recent finds listed include bags of toys and clothes, an art easel, board games, and a Radio Flyer wagon—totally free, of course! Check www.freecycle.com to see if you can participate locally.

3. **Craigslist.** The advantage of Craigslist.com over other sources of classified ads is that goods are pictured and sellers are accessible by e-mail. It can take time to hunt down the best deals, but you can search comfortably, finding amazing bargains while lounging on the couch in your pajamas. Jen scored a $100 Pottery Barn rug for just $10 by inquiring whether the seller would take a bit less than her posted price.

There are also items offered at no cost in the free section, which often is filled with good stuff on Sunday and Monday mornings after garage sales. If you've been waiting months and haven't found what you need for a reasonable price, you can also post a want ad for free in the baby and kids section. When you see something you want, e-mail immediately and get there quickly. Be aware that some sellers have an inflated view of their merchandise's value, so you'll need to compare prices carefully. We found some pieces of equipment for less at consignment shops. (See the price comparison chart later in the chapter.)

4. **Garage Sales.** When Amy Dacyczyn, author of *The Tightwad Gazette Journal,* found herself unexpectedly pregnant with twins, she hit the garage sales. She managed to spend just fifty dollars gearing up for her babies' first year—and that includes diapers! Garage sales are more time intensive than Freecycle or Craigslist, but if you find the right sale, you can get lots of gear at once and pay 50 percent less than you would at a thrift or consignment store.

Scan the paper (or look online) for sales in your area that include baby or children's items. Then get there early and remember that the seller will often be willing to negotiate on prices. Neighborhood sales or church yard sales offer a tremendous selection and may mark everything down dramatically in the afternoon. If you live in a colder climate, garage sales are seasonal, so you'll want to hit them during the spring and summer if possible.

5. **Thrift Stores.** Once thought of as a venue just for low-income shoppers, thrift stores have become mainstream for all walks of life, including hipsters, penny-pinchers, and tree-huggers. Thrift stores have the advantage of being cheaper than consignment stores, although they are not as selective with their merchandise. Check around for the place that seems to have the best-quality baby items for reasonable prices. Some may not carry baby gear because of liability issues, but keep them in mind for clothing, bibs, dishes, and toys. Often buying at a thrift store allows you to support work-training programs, faith organizations, or other local charities. You may even be able to find one whose profits support an environmental cause.

6. **Consignment Shops.** Families who don't have time for the previous options usually enjoy the convenience of a baby consignment store. It's a one-stop used gear shop that has quality merchandise available at great prices. Beyond the fact that you are reusing, you are also buying locally, supporting small businesses, limiting fuel costs (products don't have to be shipped to the store), and building community. Search your area for

shops and ask what days they buy merchandise, and then plan to visit them the following day since that is when they have the most in stock.

A decent baby resale store has a range of products available and will be a great resource as your baby outgrows things. You can sell his or her clothes for store credit and use the shop as a "gear library" as you purchase goods. If you trade wisely, you could even manage to outfit your children for almost nothing until they hit their teens! Jen's expert advice is, "If you're not planning on trading in a consignment store, the prices on clothing will sometimes be higher than buying an item new. The best bet for consignment shops are shoes, especially rubber boots and girls' dress shoes."

7. **eBay.** If you are looking for something specific for baby that can't be found elsewhere, consider searching eBay (www.ebay.com). After becoming a member, you have the opportunity to bid on merchandise for sale around the country. While the environmental and financial cost of shipping (sometimes across the country) isn't ideal, buying on eBay still has less impact than buying new. To reduce the expense of shipping, buy clothing in large lots and, if possible, buy at the end of the season for the following year to save even more.

Reselling Your Baby's Belongings: A Money-Making Venture

Sandy Choi from Brooklyn, New York, has perfected a no-cost method for using quality furniture. Years ago she found a Danish Modern sideboard in a resale shop for $500. She forked over the cash without a second thought and happily used it for quite some time. When she decided to move across the country, she put it up for sale. Her asking price? Five hundred dollars. Within a few days, the piece was sold. Quality used gear retains its value, so you can often recoup 100 percent (or more) of the cost once you're finished with it.

Rebecca, in an environmentally reckless moment, purchased a depressingly ordinary laminate chest of drawers from Target for $100. Just a year later, she saw the same exact dresser for sale used for just $20. Because of its inferior quality and design, it will only continue to decrease in value as time goes by.

Now, the moral of the story is *not* to purchase all of the most expensive baby accoutrements under the delusion that you will make most of your money back once you resell them. But resale value is a factor worth considering when you buy for baby. Some items and brands are sought-after by bargain hunters and will fetch you a fine price after you're done using them, whereas others will not. Remember, also, that a well-made baby contraption can be used by several babies over a number of years, whereas cheap things fall apart and go straight to the landfill.

You can resell your baby's possessions by hosting your own garage sale, posting an ad in a newspaper or online service, or selling goods to a consignment shop. Consignment shops will often offer you a certain percentage of its value (40 to 60 percent is typical), so if they sell your Pack-N-Play for $38, you will make about $15 to $20. You may make quite a bit more money by selling high-ticket items yourself, but it requires you to post an ad and arrange for people to come visit. This is not worth the hassle for some people but is an amusing money-making venture for others.

 Eco-nomical Tip

If you buy new gear and resell it you'll lose at least 50 percent of its value. Buying used gear and reselling it afterward, however, will keep a helpful product out of the landfill and allow you to recoup far more of your original costs, especially if the item is high quality.

The following chart shows the prices of a few typical pieces of baby equipment. Prices will vary depending on the shops you use, the percentage offered by various consignment stores, and the desirability of the merchandise you are trying to sell in your area. Cloth diapers, for example, have a very high resale value in Portland, Oregon, but may be hard to get rid of in places where they are less popular. If you don't have access to local markets for your quality resale items, consider using eBay to auction them off to buyers from across the nation.

Buying and Selling Baby's Wares: Price Comparisons

SAMPLE ITEM	NEW RETAIL PRICE	SALES PRICE IN A CONSIGNMENT SHOP (THAT OFFERS SELLERS 40%)	SALES PRICE AN INDIVIDUAL OFFERS IN AN AD
Evenflo Swing	$90	$30 (seller gets $12)	$60
Pack-N-Play	$80	$38 ($15.20)	$30–$40
Baby Bjorn	$80	$15 ($6)	$25
Graco high chair	$80	$16 ($6.40)	$15
Fisher Price Bouncer	$35	$10 ($4)	$20
Robeez shoes	$26	$10 ($4)	$8–$14
Baby Gap jeans	$25	$7 ($2.80)	$6
Chinese prefold cloth diaper	$1.25 each	$1.00 ($.40)	$1

Safety Concerns with Used Gear

There are a few things parents hesitate to buy used, no matter how eco-conscious or thrifty they may be. Safety is a valid issue, but some baby guides will tell you that you must buy certain items new. We will provide you with specific safety precautions, so that you can make your own informed decision.

SAFETY CONCERNS WITH USED CAR SEATS

Although many parents don't feel comfortable purchasing a used car seat, it is possible to find a gently used seat that will keep your baby safe and your wallet full. We don't recommend getting a car seat from a stranger or from a thrift shop, but borrowing or buying one from a trusted friend or relative can be a safe option if you follow the guidelines we've adapted from the American Academy of Pediatrics' Web site (www.aap.org). You want to know that the car seat has been well cared for, hasn't ever been in an accident, is relatively new, and hasn't been recalled. (See chapter 2 for more discussion on car seats.)

SAFETY CONCERNS WITH USED CRIBS

Many safety advocates plainly state that you should never buy a used crib—even from your best friend. Of course, previously owned cribs could be damaged, assembled incorrectly, or recalled by the factory. Safety advocates sometimes neglect to consider that new cribs could also conceivably have any of these issues. Families were shocked by the recent recall of Graco and Simplicity cribs, which was the second largest crib recall in our nation's history. Although the first infant death occurred in April 2005, the product wasn't recalled until two more babies died over the course of the next two and a half years. The deaths may have been caused by incorrect assembly, which can happen with a new or used crib.

Safety Guidelines for Used Car Seats

(These guidelines have been adapted from those set by the American Academy of Pediatrics)

Check the following aspects of a used car seat:

LABEL - The seat must have a label so that you can check the year of manufacture and ensure that the seat hasn't been recalled.

AGE - The label on the car seat should list its year of manufacture. You can then check how many years the seat can be used by going online to find the manufacturer's recommendation. Most seats are recommended for up to five years of use.

CRACKS - If you see any fissures in the plastic frame of the car seat, it could endanger your child's safety. The plastic core of the car seat should be completely without cracks.

INSTRUCTIONS - If the seat doesn't come with an instruction manual, see if you can find it online through the manufacturer. It's critical that you know how to install and operate the car seat properly.

MISSING PARTS - Ensure that all the necessary parts are intact or that you can get the missing parts from the manufacturer. (Remember that those missing parts may be expensive to order.)

SHIELD BOOSTER - Don't use a car seat with a shield booster. Although they sound like something out of Star Wars, shield boosters are a large armlike contraption that rotates down over baby's chest and shoulders. Mainly found in older car seats, shield boosters have caused injuries in children and are not recommended for use.

RECALLS - If the seat has been recalled, you can sometimes fix it by getting the proper parts. Or just pass it up if it seems unsafe. Please use the information on the label of the car seat to ensure that it was never recalled by contacting the manufacturer. Otherwise you can contact either organization below:

- Auto Safety Hot Line: Toll-free: (888) 327-4236; 8:00 a.m.–10:00 p.m. EST, Monday–Friday

- National Highway Traffic Safety Administration (NHTSA) www-odi.nhtsa.dot.gov/cars/problems/recalls/childseat.cfm

Crib Safety Guidelines

(Adapted from the American Academy of Pediatrics)

🌷 Look at the bottom of the crib to find the Juvenile Product Manufacturers Association (JPMA) certification.

🌷 If you can fit a soda can between a crib's slats, they are too wide to be safe for baby. The maximum width between slats should be 2⅜ inches.

🌷 Make sure the wood is totally smooth and free from splinters. Also check to ensure that all parts fit together perfectly.

🌷 Paint on the crib should be free of any peeling or chipping. Stay away from painted cribs manufactured earlier than 1978, since that is when lead-based paints were banned in the United States.

🌷 Check to make sure that the end panels are solid without decorative cutouts that could trap baby's head.

🌷 The four posts on the crib should either be the same height as the end panels or extremely tall like the posts on a canopy bed. Otherwise clothing or ribbons can wrap around posts and present a strangling risk.

🌷 When the crib sides are lowered, they should be at least 9 inches above the mattress. If they aren't, an infant could easily roll out of the crib. Raised crib sides should be 26 inches above the mattress when they are up in their lowest position.

🌷 The crib sides should have a lock that only an adult can release to lower them. Raise and lower it several times to ensure that the lock is sturdy.

🌷 Check that the mattress is exactly the same size as the crib without any gaps on any side. You shouldn't be able to fit two fingers between the mattress and the side of the crib. This will ensure that baby won't be able to get his arms, legs, or body trapped between the mattress and crib.

Whatever your family decides to purchase, assemble carefully using your own common sense. Check the moving parts, jiggle the bars, and innovate your own methods for ensuring that the crib is sturdy and solid. If you do choose to buy used, you can follow our safety guidelines, which are based on those set out by the American Academy of Pediatrics. You'll save a few trees and potentially hundreds of dollars.

We both own used cribs. Joy found hers on Craigslist and spoke with the previous owners, examined it carefully before the purchase, and looked at the factory name and model number online to make sure that it was never recalled. She bought the crib after she had seen it fully assembled and checked to be sure that it was sturdy and had all the necessary parts. Avoid buying used disassembled cribs unless the owner is willing to put it together for you, preferably in your presence, to be sure that every spring, bolt, and screw is accounted for. If the crib appears sound but the assembly directions are lost, you can usually find a copy of them online. Check before you purchase!

SAFETY CONCERNS WITH USED HIGH CHAIRS

New, mainstream high chairs can cost more than a hundred dollars, but they are easy to find used for about fifteen bucks. The most important thing to look for when buying a high chair is the safety restraints. The high chair should have either a T-bar that fits between the baby's legs in addition to a waist strap *or* two straps, one that goes between the baby's legs and another around the waist. Many used high chairs are missing straps and rely on the baby being held in by the tray alone. This is very dangerous; do not put a child in a high chair without the proper restraints. Some children have slid underneath the trays and been injured or, in some instances, even killed. If the high chair appears relatively new, it may be possible to call the manufacturer and replace the missing straps.

High chairs, used or new, may tumble over if the base isn't wide enough. Babies can push or kick themselves away from the kitchen table and topple over, so seek out a sturdy high chair. Be aware that old, wooden high chairs may contain lead paint. Also, as with any used product, be careful to check for missing screws or parts. The tray should lock on securely. If you are not confident that the chair you're considering is safe, pass it up.

How Can I Tell If a Toy Is Safe?

After two million Thomas the Tank Engine toys were recalled in 2007, many parents assumed they'd been pulled from store shelves. They were shocked to learn that a week after the recall notices were sent to stores, investigators walked right in and purchased the offending products. So how do you protect your kids from recalled toys? Log on to Consumer Product Safety Commission's Web site at www.cpsc.gov and subscribe to receive recall notices. The Web site contains pictures of recalled merchandise. You can also call CPSC's toll-free number to ask about specific products: (800) 638-2772.

When shopping for used toys, look for the manufacturer's name. You can either call the company directly to ask about recalls or look for it on CPSC's site. If it's unclear who made the toy or where it came from, consider leaving it behind.

The Real Cost of a Bargain: Toys from China

When expecting a bright and shiny baby, it can be tempting to opt for all-new products. Merchandise on store shelves is more alluring than garage sale offerings and sometimes can be purchased for just a few dollars. With the United States increasingly importing goods from the world market, costs are at all-time lows. But the massive product recalls on imported goods from China are a poignant reminder that bargains often come at a price. Parents in America are concerned about safety implications for their own children as continued reports of lead-based paint surface, but there is also a danger to the children of China.

According to an article in the *New York Times*, China is suffering extreme environmental challenges in its struggle to become a leading industrial power. Joseph Kahn reports of children in Chinese cities dying from pollution and lead exposure. "Environmental woes that might be considered catastrophic in some countries can seem commonplace in China," he writes. In an interview with NPR, *New York Times* China correspondent David Barboza points out that there is "an environmental cost overseas" for the super-cheap bargains on our store shelves.

Another Green Idea: Making Your Own Baby Supplies

Anyone with crafty talents may consider making baby gear instead of buying it. Knitting baby booties and hats, piecing a quilt, and assembling baby scrap books—once considered "grandma activities"—have all regained popularity as pastimes for younger generations. Making your own stuff can be a green option because your creations are more likely to become treasured heirlooms than wind up in a landfill. Even if your knitting skills aren't topnotch, your child will grow up to appreciate the time and effort you put into a little sweater or hat. When you make your own things, you can choose green materials for projects, whether you assemble something out of old objects (making a quilt out of worn-out clothes, for example) or make an effort to find new sustainable materials. See the end of this chapter for a complete list of resources for making your own gear.

Save Space, Save Money, and Save the Planet

By reducing your needs, buying used, and making your own baby memorabilia, you will enjoy many secondary benefits, such as:

✿ Less stuff in your living space

✿ More money for family trips, baby's college fund, and other upcoming expenses

✿ A planet with a few less hunks of plastic to slowly digest

By modeling recycling and reusing for your children, you will demonstrate what you really value. Instead of building memories at mega-shopping centers, your children can grow up appreciating each special toy they own, finding treasures in local garage sales, and getting to know the world they inhabit.

Embarking on Your Own Crafty Pursuits

SEWING

Green Ideas

Use pieces of fabric you already have that may otherwise be discarded as rags or look for new material made out of organic fibers.

Sewing Projects

✿ **Quilts**

✿ **Diaper bags**

✿ **Nursery decorations** including crib bumpers, wall hangings, curtains, diaper changing pad, cross-stitch and other needlework projects

✿ **Slings and other baby carriers**

✿ **Diapers and diaper covers**

✿ **Diaper wipes.** Old T-shirts or flannel receiving blankets can be made into cloth wipes by simply cutting them to the appropriate size—no hemming or sewing necessary. Keep the wipes in a pile next to the diapers, and wet them with plain water (stored in a squeezable bottle). After use, toss the wipes in the diaper pail and wash them along with the cloth diapers. If making your own wipes prevents you from buying two eighty-pack cartons of commercial wipes each month, you will not only keep seventy-two plastic cartons and 5,760 paper wipes from a landfill, but you will save almost $300 in three years!

✿ **Baby clothes**

✿ **Cloth toys**

Resources

❁ **www.diaperjungle.com** has many tips on sewing diapers and diaper covers as well as pattern resources.

❁ **www.sleepingbaby.net/jan/Baby** is a part of a Web site by Jan Andrea, a work-at-home mother who offers many patterns for making all types of baby carriers.

There are dozens of sewing books and patterns available. Here are just a few titles:

❁ *Kwik Sew's Sewing for Baby* by Kerstin Martensson

❁ *Sew & Go Baby: A Collection of Practical Baby Gear Projects* by Jasmine Hubble

❁ *Baby Couture* by Samantha McNesby

❁ *Everything for Baby: Projects to Make Yourself* by Adelaide D'Andigne

❁ *Baby Gifts: Simple Heirlooms to Make and Give* by Ethel Brennan

KNITTING

Green Ideas

Seek out yarns made out of natural, renewable fibers. Old sweaters can be felted by washing them in hot water and made into something for the baby.

Knitting Projects

❁ **Baby clothes**

❁ **Baby blankets**

❁ **Wool mattress pads**

❁ **Diaper items** including covers and "wool soakers"

Resources

Check out the Web sites on page 65 for knit diaper instructions, or read the following books to get you started:

- ✿ *Essential Baby* by Debbie Bliss
- ✿ *Expectant Knitter* by Marie Connolly
- ✿ *Knitting for Baby* by Melanie Falick and Kristin Nicholas

WORKING WITH PAPER

Green Ideas

Think about using recycled paper and nontoxic glues for paper projects.

Paper Projects

- ✿ **Mobiles.** Mobiles can be made by tying anything to sticks with string. Rebecca made a mobile with twigs, buttons, thick colored paper, and raffia she had lying around the house. It turned out beautifully and kept her from shelling out forty bucks for one at a big baby store. Be sure that all parts are carefully fastened to your homemade mobile to avoid choking hazards, and hang it out of baby's reach.

- ✿ **Wall decorations.** Drawings, paintings, collages, and paper cuttings can all function as artwork to grace baby's walls.

- ✿ **Scrap books and photo albums.** Bookmaking supplies can be found at most arts and crafts supply shops.

WOODWORKING

Green Ideas

Consider making new furnishings out of old furniture—but be careful to avoid any pieces that may contain leaded paint. Also look for wood products made out of recycled timber or wood certified by the Forest Stewardship Council to ensure that it comes from properly managed forests. Sustainable wood will be marked with the FSC label. You can find it even in national chains such as Home Depot or Lowe's.

Woodworking Projects

⚙ **Cribs** and other furniture for baby

⚙ **Rocking chairs**

⚙ **Shelves**

⚙ **Toys, blocks**

Resources

⚙ *Woodworking Projects for Women: 16 Easy-to-Build Projects for the Home and Garden* by Linda Hendry

⚙ *30 Toy Vehicles of Wood* by Ronald D. Tarjany

⚙ *Making Heirloom Toys* by Jim Makowicki

⚙ *Marvelous Transforming Toys: With Complete Instructions and Plans* by Jim Makowicki

⚙ *Tremendous Toy Trucks: With Step-by-Step Instructions and Plans for Building 12 Trucks* by Les Neufeld

4

Gearing Up Green: Supporting Eco-Friendly Companies

If you're feeling even the least bit nervous about your green consumer skills, fear not! This chapter is designed to give you everything you need to confidently select green products that fit your eco-values and your budget. Buying used is undeniably the least expensive and most environmentally friendly way to shop for a new arrival—but is it possible to purchase *new* green baby items without breaking the bank? Absolutely!

Here's what you'll find in this chapter:

⚙ The two most important items to buy green

⚙ Eco-slang—and how to understand it

⚙ The best bargains on new, eco-baby gear with heirloom, midrange, and economy options

⚙ The low-down on toxins found in bottles, mattresses, and plastic toys

The Top Three Shopping Habits of Green-Savvy Expecting Parents:

1. Instead of opting to purchase every item new, the wise parent-to-be finds plenty of resale deals, picks out a few new green favorites, and drops not-so-subtle hints whenever friends and family are nearby.

2. These folks use duct tape, string, and decoupage to creatively reuse what they have—with mixed results. Then they have plenty of money left over for their green splurges.

3. Using a fluent eco-vocabulary and a greenwashing radar, these shoppers confidently stroll past consumer traps set to ensnare the uninformed but well-intentioned eco-consumer.

Thankfully it's easier than ever to find green goods. Eco-friendly baby products are popping up on the shelves of local businesses and even big-box stores because as eco-conscious consumers, each purchase we make is influencing manufacturers to shift to our demands—and our green dollars are working! As organic and sustainable items become more widely available, they don't always cost much more than buying mainstream goods. And with the help of economic offsetting, it's possible to budget for those green items that are a bit more expensive.

Here's how economic offsetting works: In addition to finding creative ways to limit your environmental impact, you hunt for room in your budget to offset costlier eco-friendly items. For example, using secondhand clothing for baby can help you set aside hundreds of dollars for an organic crib mattress or an heirloom crib crafted from responsibly harvested hardwoods.

What about the family who's already shopping at thrift stores, growing their own food, and using hand-me-downs? Or the single parent who is working three jobs to make ends meet? There may not be a way to offset very tight budgets, but if you're interested in extreme savings, check out Amy Dacyczyn's *Tightwad Gazette*. After reading it, you may be motivated to go for home haircuts, container gardening, and other creative ideas for cutting back so you can afford a few green splurges.

Before you spend baby's college fund on all our high-end recommendations, please be sure to read chapters 2 and 3. In reality, baby needs very little, and you can find most of it used. Since neither of us green cheapskates spent more than one thousand dollars on baby's entire first year, you'll quickly deduce that we didn't buy many expensive products. We'll give you a range of green options that offer good values for the price.

Top Two Items to Buy New

MATTRESSES

Beyond the sanitary concerns of used mattresses, studies have shown that babies who sleep on previously used ones are at a higher risk for SIDS (*Tappin-British Medical Journal*). We believe it's worth the investment to purchase a new eco-friendly crib mattress because of the toxins in mainstream mattresses. Should you consider a used, organic mattress? Only if you feel comfortable that it's been carefully stored and well cared for.

BOTTLES

Unless you're able to get your hands on a quality set of used glass bottles, it's really best to purchase them new. Plastic bottles can contain toxins that leach as the bottles break down.

Green Moms Think Outside the Box Springs

"After doing the research, I realized that there was no way I would want my little baby sleeping in a toxic bed. My mother bought his mattress as a gift from organicgrace.com for around $200 (shipping was free). We've only been pleased with it. It is made out of 100 percent organic cotton and wool and has springs in it. I've heard that for children with wool sensitivity, latex mattresses are a better choice (although a bit pricier).

"We don't have problems with wool, which is why we also opted for wool puddle pads instead of a traditional mattress cover (most of which are made of PVC and off-gas toxic chemicals continuously). Wool pads are ridiculously expensive, so I cut up a hefty wool camping blanket we never used and made a crib pad, a bassinet pad, and two changing table pads out of the one blanket. I lanolized the entire lot and have never had any problems with leaks. We also use organic sheets (which I bought used on eBay for half the new price).

"It's really easy to be overwhelmed with the number of hazardous everyday baby items most people willingly buy and think they have to have. We make a focused effort to follow Thoreau's advice to 'Simplify, simplify, simplify!' The less stuff you have, the less you have to worry about. We opt out of most of the gadgety baby items, which leaves more money for buying the quality safer necessities."

DOROTHY HALL, Siloam Springs, Arkansas

"To save money (and space) I bought my daughter a 'mini crib' before she was born and an organic mattress to go with it. Because it's a smaller crib, the mattress cost less. Here's where I bought mine—www.naturalemporium.com— and so far, I've been very pleased."

KIRSTEN AADAHL, New York City, New York

How to Lanolize

Lanolizing is an easy and natural way to make wool or other fabrics water-resistant. Heat one cup of water and then add one teaspoon lanolin. (Lanolin is easily purchased in tubes and often used to soothe sore nipples in those first days of breastfeeding.) Stir until it dissolves and then soak the wool item in the lanolin solution for fifteen minutes. Remove the item from the solution but don't rinse. Just roll in a towel to soak up excess moisture and lay flat to dry.

Green Product Recommendations

In this section you'll find several dozen companies that create quality green products for your child. We'll always list heirloom products first, which may sound surprising coming from a couple of green skinflints. Why would we even list the most expensive products? Because if you're going to buy new, investing in high-quality gear will have the least environmental impact. An heirloom toy will be used by generations of babies because of the quality of its construction and workmanship, whereas cheaply made gear will hit the landfill within a few years. And remember that you'll be able to resell high-end equipment for a good amount after baby is finished with it. In the company selections we list, we honestly believe "you get what you pay for."

The prices we quote may change with time, so please double check the Web sites before you outline your budget with specific numbers.

CRIB MATTRESSES

Crib mattresses are the first item listed for a reason—they are the most important item to purchase new and organic. While conventional mattresses are cheaper, they are made out of foam, vinyl, and several other by-products of petroleum. These ingredients harm the environment while they're manufactured and have been linked to health risks as well. Since an infant will spend up to sixteen hours a day snoozing on a crib mattress, it's worth the money to find a safer alternative.

If you still don't feel like an organic mattress is in the budget (after all, you can get a conventional crib mattress for just $50), here are some ideas some of our green-babyguide.com readers came up with:

❧ If you plan to sleep with your child, look into an adult-size organic mattress and skip the crib mattress altogether. This is not only healthier for the whole family, but greener because while a crib mattress gets used for just a couple years, adults hang on to their mattresses much longer.

❧ Look into a mini-crib instead of a normal-size crib—the smaller mattress will cost less money, so an organic one will be more affordable.

❧ Use a conventional mattress—but look for an organic wool or cotton mattress cover.

❧ Look for an organic cotton futon crib mattress. These don't contain foam.

What to Look For

It's important to find standard-size crib mattresses that will fit tightly into a normal crib and are quite firm. (SIDS risks increase on extremely soft mattresses.) Some organic crib mattresses aren't fire retardant and thus require a signed note from a physician to comply with federal fire safety standards. However, since the risk of household fire is much higher than the risks associated with using a traditional mattress, we recommend organic mattresses that use wool, which is naturally flame retardant enough to meet safety standards.

PBDEs: Toxic Baby Mattresses

All mainstream mattresses (and baby bedding) are treated with fire-retardant polybrominated diphenyl ethers (PBDEs). Most are filled with polyurethane foam—a highly flammable material sometimes called "solid gasoline" by fire fighters. According to an Environment California Research and Policy Center study, PBDE chemicals have been found in the bloodstream of American children and babies at three times the amount found in adults. Europe has already banned the use of some types of PBDEs. If you aren't able to buy a PBDE-free mattress, air out the standard crib gear as much as possible before using.

What to Avoid

Some mainstream brands claim to have organic components, but aren't completely eco-friendly. Stick to all-organic options if you're going to splurge for a green mattress.

Heirloom Picks

While it's nice to buy high-quality baby furniture or clothes that can be handed down, used mattresses are the exception since they're associated with an elevated SIDS risk. For this reason, we don't have any heirloom picks for mattresses.

Midrange Options

✿ **The Natural Rubber Organic Crib Mattress** by Absolutely Organic Baby
   (www.absolutelyorganicbaby.com) $390
   Made from rubber, organic cotton, and organic wool. The mattress is naturally flame retardant without chemical additives.

✿ **242 Coil Organic Cotton and Organic Ecowool mattress** by Nirvana
   Safe Haven (www.nontoxic.com) $349
   Offers an organic cotton and wool mattress that is naturally flame retardant and free of synthetic materials.

✿ **The No-Compromise Organic Cotton Classic** by Naturepedic
   (www.naturepedic.com) $259
   This mattress offers a waterproof surface made from food-grade polyethylene, an organic cotton filling, firm support, and a nontoxic fire protection system.

Economy Choices

✿ **The Refill Mattress** by Pixel Organics
   (www.pixelorganics.com) $170
   The core of this mattress is made from food-grade polyethylene fibers from discarded bottles. It's then wrapped in organic cotton and wool and covered with a washable organic cover.

CRIBS

What to Look For

The eco-friendliest cribs are made from sustainable wood products that come from carefully managed forests. Stains should be nontoxic and/or made from natural oils. Hardwoods are more expensive but will hold up better over the years as the crib is passed on to other babies. If possible, buy a crib that comes from Forest Stewardship Council certified wood. The Forest Stewardship Council was established in 1992 at the Earth Summit in Rio de Janeiro to define standards and certification processes for sustainable forestry. Look for FSC-certified labels on cribs, baby furniture, and even wood purchased from your local hardware store. The label ensures that wood is harvested, treated, and manufactured using sustainable practices.

What to Avoid

Fiberboard or medium-density fiberboard (MDF) is made from a composite of glued wood chips and covered with a veneer. MDF contains formaldehyde and can off-gas for years. Some "green" cribs are made from recycled wood fibers that are made into fiberboard. Make sure to check that the glues used to bond the fibers is nontoxic for baby if you're interested in a recycled wood crib.

Heirloom Picks

✿ **Arts and Crafts Style Crib** by Pacific Rim Woodworking
(www.pacificrimwoodworking.com) $700
These organic cribs offer a great value and superb quality. Pacific Rim cribs are made from FSC-certified solid maple. The cribs are finished with beeswax and tung oil and can be converted into toddler beds. This is the only FSC-certified crib we found for less than a thousand dollars. It's American made and the wood is sustainably harvested from the coastal forests of Oregon.

Midrange Options

⚙ Amish Made Americana Crib

(www.thecleanbedroom.com) $495

This oak crib is built by Amish craftsmen in Ohio and finished with tung oil. The crib rails don't move, but the mattress can be adjusted up or down as baby grows.

⚙ European-Style Solid Wood Crib

(www.greenearthmarket.com) $495

Another Amish-crafted crib made from oak and finished with a nontoxic stain. The crib can be easily converted to a toddler bed as well.

Economy Choices

⚙ Alpha 3-in-1 Crib

(www.babyearth.com) $160

It's possible to buy a crib made from sustainably managed oak for less than $200! While the price is thrilling, the downside is that the Alpha crib is made in China with wood imported from New Zealand. Granted, the wood is harvested responsibly, but your crib will log several hundred miles before it reaches baby's nursery. Still, if your budget is limited and you'd like a hardwood option with nontoxic stain, it's nice to know there's a green(er) option.

 Eco-nomical Tip

In the long run, buying quality will save you money and environmental impact. We know a mother of five who bought a low-quality crib for her first child and then had to replace it three times for the following four children. She ended up spending as much as she would have on an eco-friendly crib and sending a total of four cribs to the landfill!

Dictionary of Eco-Slang

There are so many issues to consider when buying eco-friendly baby gear. How can you tell a product is authentically good for baby and the environment with all the labels out there?

ORGANIC – A cotton crop might be certified as organic by the USDA but can then be loaded down with chemical finishes or toxic dyes when it is processed into a garment, toy, or baby blanket. Look for an Organic Trade Association certification if you're going to go organic. The OTA ensures that textiles are grown, woven, dyed, and sewn in an environmentally responsible manner.

FAIR-TRADE – Fair-trade certified goods pay workers in other countries livable wages, allow them to unionize, avoid child labor, and ensure that no harsh or inhumane treatment is allowed. Try to ensure that the imported baby gear you purchase is "Fair Trade Certified."

AMERICAN MADE – It's always nice to know that the product you purchase hasn't toured the globe before arriving at your doorstep. In fact, buying something made in the USA is clearly greener than buying a fair-trade certified item from afar. (Even better—try to find things handmade in your own community!)

NATURAL – This claim doesn't mean much. Since there's no certification process for "natural" products, don't put too much stock in this label. Items may be made from natural wood, metal, or cloth, but that doesn't mean it's been manufactured or finished in an eco-friendly manner.

GREENWASHING – To cut costs and still meet the needs of the eco-friendly con-sumer, many companies are becoming experts at "greenwashing." A product may be labeled organic or fair trade, but take the claims with a grain of salt. We've taken care in this chapter to double check the environmental claims of all our recommendations.

NURSERY FURNITURE

What to Look For

You'll want to search for other nursery furniture products made from solid wood, prefer-ably hardwoods, that are finished with natural stains. There are also several brands that use MDF made from recycled wood fibers and nontoxic, formaldehyde-free resins. Consider pieces that are flexible—for example, a dresser that will double as a changing table and last well into baby's childhood.

What to Avoid

Standard particleboard, plywood, and pressboard all use glues that can contain urea-formaldehyde resins. Furniture made from these materials is typically quite a bit cheaper than solid wood pieces but isn't as eco-friendly or as safe as buying green or buying used.

Heirloom Picks

✿ The Q Collection Junior

(www.qcollectionjunior.com) $1000+

While the Q Collection is rather expensive, it does offer extremely good-quality products that meet all possible eco-standards. It has achieved GreenGuard certification, is nontoxic, formaldehyde free, and uses low VOC paints.

Midrange Options

✿ Celery

(www.celeryfurniture.com) $200–1000

Celery's sleek, eco-friendly designs have been mentioned in the *New York Times* and spotted on the *Today Show*. Made from formaldehyde-free particleboard and bamboo, its furniture is decorated with low-VOC paint and finishes.

Economy Picks

✿ The Green Lullaby

(www.green-lullaby.com) $50–100

This incredibly creative company makes dollhouses, playhouses, and even an eco-cradle (for baby to sleep in!) out of reinforced and recycled cardboard that's been fire-proofed with eco-friendly ingredients.

CLOTHING

What to Look For

Check to make sure that the product contains 100 percent certified organic cotton that hasn't been bleached or dyed with harsh chemicals. If the business has an Organic Trade Association label on its Web page, you can be sure that the processing of organic cotton is handled just as responsibly as the farming.

What to Avoid

Although ultrasoft synthetic blankets and soothies have become quite popular in recent years, organic polyester doesn't exist! Organic cotton, hemp, and wool are the best options for baby. Bamboo is controversial—read the sidebar for more info.

Heirloom Picks

As thrift store connoisseurs, we simply cannot bring ourselves to recommend that you spend hundreds of dollars on baby fashions or bedding. Stick to the midrange prices and you'll still find high-quality garments that will last through many a newborn's infancy.

Midrange Options

✿ Hanna Andersson
(www.hannaandersson.com) $14–30
Made of thick, high-quality cotton inspired by Swedish fabrics, Hanna Andersson clothes are certain to last through several babies. Not every piece is organic, but there is a wide variety of organic options.

✿ My Little Pakora
(www.mylittlepakora.com) $12–30
This company combines Indian style and eco-friendly values with luxurious organic fabrics. Its clothes are both comfortable and durable with many styles to choose from.

⚙ Speesees

(www.speesees.com) $15–50

The bright colors and bold designs of Speesees make its line of clothing especially fun. The company's motto, "We're all in this together," reflects its environmental commitment.

Bamboo—A Green Choice?

There have been several claims made about bamboo fabric and many of them are true, but several others aren't quite accurate.

FACTS

- Since bamboo is a species of grass, it's a fast-growing crop that can be quickly raised without too many pesticides or herbicides.

- Compared with cotton, bamboo requires far less water.

- Because most bamboo is grown in Asia, it then logs thousands of miles before it hits our shores, emitting a lot of carbon dioxide in the process.

MYTHS

- *Bamboo is grown and harvested sustainably.* In fact, bamboo is a huge business for farmers in China and because of this, many forests have been cut down to raise it. Most land belongs to private companies and is not regulated for sustainable farming practices.

- *Bamboo fabric is antibacterial and protects skin from UV rays.* In a University of Colorado study, scientists showed that both of these claims were in fact false.

- *Processing bamboo from plant to fabric is eco-friendly.* Many of the chemicals used to break the cellulose-based plant into fibers aren't eco-friendly.

Economy Choices

✿ **Organic Gerber Onesies**

(www.gerber.com/products) $9.99–14

Gerber's four-pack of organic onesies is a true tightwad bargain.

✿ **Organic Selections at Big Box Stores**

Babies R Us, Target, and WalMart now carry several certified organic items for baby at very reasonable prices. An organic cotton thermal receiving blanket can be purchased at Babies R Us for just $8.99!

BOTTLES

What to Look For

Glass bottles offer the safest option, both for baby's health and the environment. If plastic is still more appealing to you, there are several safer plastics to choose from.

What to Avoid

Stay away from clear, rigid plastics that haven't been labeled BPA-free. Also, be sure that you buy new baby bottles if you do choose plastic. Plastic tends to leach more toxins when repeatedly heated and cooled over time. Since bottles are often sterilized and frozen, it's best not to buy plastic used.

Midrange Options

✿ **Born Free Glass Bottles**

(www.newbornfree.com) $12.95 each

Born Free bottles come with silicone nipples and a vented system that helps to reduce colic and ear infections.

Note: More midrange options are available in chapter 7.

Economy Picks

✿ 6-Pack Evenflo Sensitive Response Glass Baby Bottles

(www.evenflo.com) $14.95

Designed with micro air vents to keep air from entering baby's stomach and available in 8-ounce or 4-ounce sizes.

STROLLERS

What to Look For

No one wants a stroller that's more difficult to lug around than the actual baby. Find a light, compact stroller that fits easily into your life with plenty of flexibility. Some families end up buying heavy-duty strollers, running strollers, and compact strollers. If possible, try to find one that can cover as many of your needs as possible.

What to Avoid

Stay away from bulk and plastic—especially bulky plastic! If possible, try to buy a stroller that uses metal and fabric as its key components.

Heirloom Picks

✿ Baby Bling

(www.strollerideas.com/babybling.html) $549.95

These unique strollers, designed by a small American company, are built for reuse. The metal frame is constructed in China and designed to hold a removable fabric nest for baby. When the fabric wears down, the next owner can purchase a fabric replacement from the same company.

Buy Hand-Crafted Eco-friendly Baby Gear on Etsy

Do you want unique, eco-friendly gifts for your little one that are handmade here in the USA.? What about shopping on www.etsy.com? Etsy sells wares made by crafters that are much more interesting than mass-produced stuff from big box stores. Here are some online shops worth checking out.

WARM AND FUZZY BABY - Darling organic hats, blankets, and booties

ORGANIC QUILT COMPANY - Stunning organic baby quilts for very reasonable prices

NEW ENGLAND GIFT COMPANY - Ribbon-lined organic hooded baby towels and retro-print baby blankets

LOVEY DUDS - Organic wraps to tote baby around in, plus some "hooter hiders" in colorful organic fabrics

MAIDEN LOVE - Soft flannel elephant toys stuffed with wool and organic lavender

BABUS - Soft fabric blocks made from recycled fabrics, plus some wool teethers

SIMPLE DREAMS - An ingenious little "gift pouch" for a gift certificate that can later be used to keep a lock of baby's hair or a first tooth

AGAPE LUV - Eco-friendly kimonos for baby, made from organic or recycled fabric and "solar power sewn"!

WOOLY BABY - Adorable, warm baby slippers made from recycled sweaters

Midrange Options

✿ Baby Planet

(www.baby-planet.com) $189

Many of Baby Planet's strollers are named after endangered species. The company has a stroller donation and recycling program online, and its high-quality strollers start at just $189. Plus a small portion of each sale is dedicated to environmental causes. The only drawback is that the strollers are made in China.

Economy Choices

⚙ Maclaren Strollers

(www.maclarenbaby.com) $99.99+

Maclaren strollers offer simple metal-and-fabric construction and feature a one-hand compact umbrella fold with a water-resistant canopy. Some of their less expensive strollers are suitable only for babies older than six months whereas more deluxe models will accommodate baby from birth onward. Maclaren has begun using organic materials in its strollers and ensures that its materials are lead-free and phthalate-free. It also has a recycling program for used strollers.

TOYS

What to Look For

Toys made from natural materials and nontoxic fabrics, paints, and stains are the best bet for your child. Since babies end up popping just about everything in their mouth, it's good to know that objects are safe for baby to chew on. Also, it's best to look for American-made or European-made products whenever possible.

What to Avoid

The aisles of big-box stores are teeming with brightly colored plastic toys—all of which have relatively short life spans and some of which contain harmful toxins. Since plastic is made from petroleum, its production process isn't eco-friendly. Plus plastic toys often break down faster than those made of wood or metal, and they can't biodegrade or be recycled.

Eco-nomical Tip

If you're planning on having multiple children, consider buying gender-neutral duds for your first babe. You'll be able to reuse everything with future children and can easily "accessorize" with hair bows or high tops if you want people to know your baby's gender.

Heirloom Picks

⚙ HABA

(Widely available online and in local toyshops)

HABA began making toys in Germany in 1938 and has the environment at the heart of its corporate values. Its toys have passed the strict European Environment Standard ISO 1400 that ensures that every step in the production process is eco-friendly.

⚙ Nova Natural Toys

(www.novanatural.com)

This small Vermont toy company makes hardwood toys, wooden kitchens, and a variety of other quality products for children. Its prices are fair and the range of its products is impressive.

Midrange Options

⚙ Plan Toys

(www.plantoysusa.com)

Plan Toys are made of rubberwood from rubber trees that no longer product latex. The wood is then naturally hardened by curing it in a kiln and made into toys. The products all have water-based dyes and nontoxic stains. Although the company is based in Thailand, the safety standards are very high.

⚙ Melissa and Doug Wooden Toys

(www.melissaanddoug.com)

Started in their garage in 1988, Melissa and Doug have always crafted their toys from wood or phthalate-free plastic. Their bright colors and creative designs make these items a big hit with infants and toddlers.

Economy Choices

⚙ Sassy Earth Bright Toys

(www.sassybaby.com)

Sassy's line of earth-friendly wood and fabric toys can be found at most mainstream stores for very reasonable prices. The line mainly features small items, but the toys are widely available.

Keeping Baby Safe from Environmental Toxins

Being green isn't just about protecting the earth for the future, it's also about keeping baby safe from the environment here and now. Surprisingly, many baby products available on the market today contain toxins. You may want to consider avoiding these toxins when purchasing either new or used products. Look for these labels when selecting baby products:

BPA FREE – Biphesenol-A, or BPA, has been banned in Canada because of links to health risks including cancers, impaired immune function, and diabetes. BPA is a chemical commonly found in plastics used to make flexible teethers, baby toys, and baby bottles. Although it is still approved by the FDA, BPA-free product lines are growing to meet consumer demands. For more information on BPA go to: www.environmentcalifornia.org.

PHTHALATE FREE/PVC FREE – Phthalates are a group of chemicals found in poly-vinyl chloride (PVC) plastic products and some personal care products. Many pacifiers, plastic nipples, bath books, bottles, and toys commonly contain phthalates. Also, some scented baby lotions, soaps, or other products use them to bind fragrance with the solution. These chemicals have been linked to premature birth, reproductive defects, and early-onset puberty. Again, the demand for phthalate-free products is growing, and there are now a wide variety to choose from.

OTHER ENVIRONMENTAL DANGERS

Toxins can also be found in carpet, paint, disposable diapers, synthetic cloth, cleaning supplies, and detergent. Many new parents paint the nursery, install new carpet, and use chemical cleansers in anticipation of the baby. To learn more about common toxins that could affect your baby, refer to the sources listed below:

- **For a quick overview of common baby toxins and their alternatives,** look at the Environmental Health Association of Nova Scotia's Guide to Less Toxic Products at www.lesstoxicguide.ca.

- **For more in-depth information, read** *Raising Healthy Children in a Toxic World: 101 Smart Solutions for Every Family* by Philip J. Landrigan, Herbert L. Needleman, and Mary M. Landrigan. The book contains detailed data about everyday sources of toxins in your child's life and practical solutions.

Beyond Baby: Extending Eco-Consumerism to Life in General

Warning: Buying eco-friendly products has interesting side effects. You may find yourself overwhelmed with a happy, hopeful glow that lasts for days after purchasing something as insignificant as an eco-friendly burp rag. Like saving a kitten from the treetops or writing a generous check to your favorite charity, putting your money in line with your values feels incredibly good. And like all acts of goodness, it sometimes spills into other categories of your life. You might find yourself using that eco-slang to buy products beyond the nursery. We've found that each small change we made for our babies led to bigger shifts in our consciousness and our consumerism. See our resource directory for a list of more green businesses—and thanks for investing in a greener future!

Resources

The Ultimate Green Gear Buying Guide

If you want a vast array of info on green baby gear, check out *Itsabelly's Guide to Going Green with Baby.* The book includes detailed product reviews on just about every baby product you could possibly imagine. It's available for purchase online at www.itsa-belly.com.

Other Green Companies Offering Baby Gear

✿ **Rosie Hippo**

(www.rosiehippo.com)

This small company features plenty of natural toys, rattles, and various items to outfit your green nursery.

✿ **Natural Pod**

(www.naturalpod.com)

With a focus on creative, open-ended play, Natural Pod has a wide range of products designed to allow children to use their imagination. Besides toys, the company also carries several pieces of organic clothing and even a few wooden bikes.

✿ Momma's Baby

(www.mommasbaby.com)

From your pregnancy to your cloth-diapering days, Momma's Baby has it all. You'll find breastfeeding supplies, cloth diapers, and home and health products as well. Plus, the Web site has a convenient online baby registry.

✿ Ecobaby Organics

(www.ecobaby.com)

Organic mattresses, cribs, cloth diapers, toys, and breastfeeding supplies are just some of the things you'll find on Ecobaby Organic's site. When you type in the URL, you will be directed to Pure Rest Organics, Ecobaby Organic's parent company, but the product line will be the same.

✿ Pedoodles

(www.pedoodles.com)

Pedoodles has a line of sturdy, eco-friendly baby shoes made from leather remnants.

✿ Nature's Crib

(www.naturescrib.com)

From natural furniture to organic baby bedding, Nature's Crib has a variety of organic and eco-friendly baby gear at reasonable prices.

5

The Great Diaper Dilemma:
Cloth and Disposable
Diapers Face Off

Everyone's heard the arguments about cloth and disposables, but what's really true? Chances are you don't have time to analyze research studies to find the eco-friendliest diapering option. Thanks to this chapter, you can spend the hours you would have used digging through mounds of information to play with your baby—or nap! We'll clarify which are the eco-friendliest diapering methods using the latest research and the studies we've conducted in our own washing machines.

Also in this chapter:

❁ How to "green" your cloth diapers—What's the best for the planet?

❁ Diaper services—How do they compare to disposables?

❁ The cost of cloth versus the cost of disposables—What will save you big bucks?

❁ Greener disposables on the market—Worth the higher price tag?

This chapter will reveal ways to save mounds of trash, gallons of water, and pounds of carbon dioxide—not to mention thousands of dollars—diapering your baby. If you are already convinced that cloth diapers are the way to go, turn to the next chapter for tips on choosing a cloth diapering system and advice about caring for your diapers.

A few quick diaper facts:

- The average baby will go through six thousand diaper changes before potty training.

- According to the directions on boxes of disposables, soiled diapers should be dunked in the toilet to remove solid waste before they're thrown in the trash.

- Cloth diapers today are better than ever, with Velcro closures instead of pins and without the need for plastic pants.

- No one knows how long it will take for a disposable diaper to decompose in a landfill, though some estimate as long as five hundred years. Diapers dumped there in the 1970s are still fully intact today.

In the Diaper Dumps

What's so bad about sending trash to the dump? Well, we have to consider the energy used to transport trash from your house to the landfill as well as the effects a diaper has on the planet when it breaks down. Although package instructions on disposable diapers advise flushing solid waste down the toilet before tossing the diaper in the trash, many parents wrap up the waste in the diaper. This contributes bio-hazardous waste to our landfills, which then leaks out into our water supply. Garbage also lets off greenhouse gases when it breaks down. Basically, the smellier your trash, the more harmful gases you're releasing into the atmosphere. On top of all that, almost *nothing* can break down in a landfill—including biodegradable waste like food and paper—due to the anaerobic environment of all that compacted trash. In a University of Arizona study, researchers uncovered recognizable hot dogs and corn cobs that had been in the landfill for more than twenty-five years as well as a newspaper that was still readable after fifty years in a dump. A man-made disposable diaper doesn't stand a chance!

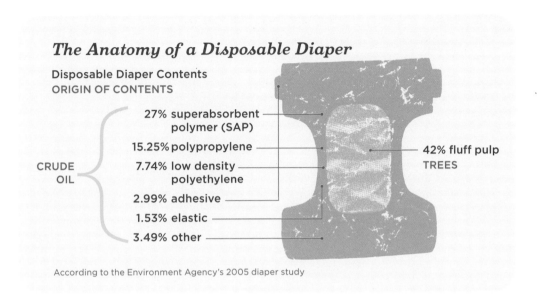

The Anatomy of a Disposable Diaper

Disposable Diaper Contents
ORIGIN OF CONTENTS

27% superabsorbent polymer (SAP)

15.25% polypropylene

7.74% low density polyethylene

2.99% adhesive

1.53% elastic

3.49% other

CRUDE OIL

42% fluff pulp
TREES

According to the Environment Agency's 2005 diaper study

93

The Debate Between Disposable and Cloth Diapers Wages On

It seemed as if we'd never find a diaper study that wasn't sponsored by a disposable diaper company . . . or a diaper service. Imagine our excitement when we found the British Environment Agency's 2005 Lifecycle Analysis (LCA) diaper study, which was updated in 2008. In a nutshell, it explains that cloth diapers take a toll on the planet because of the water and energy used to wash and dry the diapers, and disposable diapers make the biggest impact during their production and disposal.

They determined that using disposable diapers for 2.5 years would have a "global warming impact" of about 1,210 pounds of carbon dioxide equivalents. But it's possible to cut that down to just 814 pounds of carbon if you use cloth diapers and launder them with as little energy as possible.

How to Green Your Cloth Diapers

Using cloth diapers isn't always best for the environment—you still have to take care to wash them as efficiently as possible. Below you'll find some tips for greening your diaper laundry. Line-drying, for example, is a completely carbon-free activity, scoring you major eco-points. In reality you won't be able to use cloth diapers without *some* environmental impact—so look at the following ideas as possibilities, not hard-and-fast rules.

❣ Your best bet is to buy secondhand diapers (for the planet and your pocketbook!). Believe it or not, there is quite a market for previously owned cloth diapers in many cloth-diapering communities and online sites such as eBay.

❣ The second greenest option is to buy new diapers made from organically grown materials.

❣ Wash full loads of diapers. Instead of washing twelve diapers every other day, you can wash three dozen prefolds every four days for maximum efficiency or twelve to fifteen pocket diapers every three days.

❣ Wash diapers in cold water. Yes, it is possible! We discuss laundering methods in more detail in chapter 6.

❣ Use a high-efficiency machine. Instead of using up to 50 gallons a wash, as you would with a top-loader, you'd use about 12 gallons a wash. Just run one heavy cycle and avoid extra rinses.

❣ Don't soak your diapers. Just use a dry pail.

❣ Hang your diapers to dry as much as you can (see chapter 6 for more drying tips).

❣ Avoid tumble drying whenever possible.

❣ Do not iron your diapers.

❣ Save your diapers for a second child or sell them/give them away so another child can use them. Even if you buy all-new conventionally grown cotton diapers, they can be used again and again for at least two children. Joy bought sanitized, used diapers from a diaper service, then diapered her son with them and let a friend borrow them for her two children before using them again for her second child. That means at least five children (or more!) were diapered by that same set of prefolds.

If you followed every one of those tips, you could reduce your impact by as much as 33 percent over disposables!

We didn't do everything right when we started our cloth diapering odyssey. We bought used diaper covers, but Rebecca bought new cotton prefolds of dubious origins. Living in the damp and drizzly Pacific Northwest, we both used our dryers more than we'd like to admit. Still, with our front-loading washing machines, we figure we used just 1,089 gallons of water a year on diaper laundry. To put that into perspective, we'd use more than twice as much water in a year by taking a daily five-minute shower.[5]

Lifecycle of a Disposable Diaper

Now let's look at disposable diapers. Currently, 90 percent of babies in the United States wear disposable diapers, and it takes 1.3 million tons of wood pulp—or 250,000 trees—to create those diapers—not to mention 82,000 tons of plastic (according to the Rhode Island Solid Waste Management Corporation). **Since disposables are used just once and then thrown away, trees need to be cut down and plastic needs to be produced from crude oil every single day, forever and ever.**

The Environment Agency's study did not consider what would happen if everyone stopped using disposables and switched over to cloth, which they admit would "result in alternative use of the forest, be it for alternative products, alternative crops, recreational use, etc." Likewise, they did not examine possible alternative uses of cotton fields if all cloth-users switched to disposables. They state, "These secondary effects, *though likely to be significant*, are generally ignored in LCA studies." (Emphasis ours.)

....
[5] Using the U.S. Department of Interior's water usage calculator, we'd use 10 gallons of water for a
      five-minute shower, or 3,650 gallons/year.

And then there's all that garbage. According to the U.S. Environmental Protection Agency, disposable diapers create 3.4 million tons of waste, making up 2.1 percent of trash crowding the landfills in the United States. The British Environment Agency noted that "there is a lack of data describing the behavior of disposable nappies and their contents when they are disposed." Obviously, it would be hard to stick around a landfill for five hundred years examining its effects on the environment, but it's important to note that when the Environment Agency came up with its conclusions, it wasn't able to factor in the long-term effects diapers may have on the planet.

Swaddling Baby in Petroleum

The majority of the contents of a disposable diaper are made from crude oil, and with more than 90 percent of U.S. parents opting for Pampers over cloth, our country is using more than seven billion gallons of oil annually just in diapers. Since those plastic materials produced from disposables won't break down easily in landfills, we're saddling future generations with overcrowded landfills and energy shortages due to our dependence on petroleum.

The Cost of Disposable Diapers

Consumer Reports estimates that you'll spend $1,500 to 2,000 on disposable diapers before your child is potty trained. Of course, any bargain hunter or coupon clipper can figure out how to beat that average. Disposable diapers become more expensive as they get bigger in size. The following chart estimates how much you'd spend on disposables in two and a half years after going through six thousand diapers. We calculated the cost of the greener disposables on the market and included Huggies and a generic store brand for comparison's sake.

Another disposable option is gDiapers. You can buy starter packs in sizes small, medium, and large, which contain two cloth pants and ten disposable (flushable) liners.

Refill packs containing thirty-two liners are available for $13.99. Let's assume that in two and a half years of diapering, you would buy six starter packs, so that you'd have at least four pairs of cloth pants in each size. You'd then need to buy 186 refill packs for the six thousand diaper changes you'll make. You'll spend a total of $2,602.14 gDiapering your baby. This does not include the cost of flushing the inserts. You can save some money by ordering the refills by the case on their Web site. Six starter kits and forty-two cases of liners in two different sizes would cost $2,345.94 at www.gdiapers.com.

These figures do not include the cost of disposable wipes, plastic bags for individual diaper disposal, garbage bags, or trash expenses. Increased garbage service may or may not be a factor where you live. Rebecca saves $100 a year with once-a-month rather than once-a-week trash pickup because her three-person family never generates more than about 15 to 20 gallons of trash a month thanks in part to cloth diapering. If you want to get really nitpicky, you could also figure out how much extra gasoline you may end up using for those emergency grocery store runs!

Estimated Price of Disposable Diapers by Brand

BRAND	COST PER DIAPER	6,000 DIAPERS
Generic store brand	11–19 cents	$900
Huggies	19–31 cents	$1,500
Whole Foods 365 brand	26–32 cents	$1,740
Nature BabyCare*	27–40 cents	$1,980
Tushies (Tendercare)*	26–41 cents	$2,079
Seventh Generation	28–43 cents	$2,100

The average retail price of sizes 1–4 was used for these calculations.

*Tushies and Nature Baby Care diaper prices from diapers.com. Shipping costs not included. Grocery store prices were used for the other diapers.

Health Concerns with Disposable Diapers

Many parents may choose cloth diapers or greener disposable diapers out of concern for baby's health. Disposables are made from bleached tree pulp and a long list of man-made materials, but the most troubling ingredients are chlorine bleach and SAP (sodium polyacrylate, a.k.a. absorbent gel).

Conventional diapers are made from wood pulp bleached with chlorine and may contain traces of dioxin, a carcinogenic chemical that has been banned in several countries. Chlorine is also an environmental toxin. Refer to our review of greener disposables later in this chapter for chlorine-free alternatives to conventional disposables.

Many parents are concerned the presence of SAP in disposables causes the scrotal temperature of baby boys to get too high, interfering with normal sperm production. Research by the Archives of Disease in Childhood showed that the scrotal temperature is higher in boys who wear disposable diapers than in those who wear cloth, possibly explaining the increase in male infertility over the last twenty-five years.[6] Most disposables, including the greener ones, use SAP and assure parents of its safety. Try Tushies for a gel-free diaper.

The Cost of Cloth

How much does it cost to cloth diaper a child from birth to potty training? Your figure will depend on several variables, but the short answer is that it will cost whatever you spend on cloth diaper supplies (from free to $800) plus whatever you spend on laundering your cloth diapers (from $49.48 to more than $1,000 in two and a half years, depending on your methods and energy costs). Once you have purchased cloth diapering supplies, it is possible to diaper your baby for as little as $20 a year! That means you could diaper a second child for just *fifty* bucks. If you have two children, this results in a savings of more than $1,500 over the very cheapest disposables we found.

[6] Partsch, Aukamp, and Sippell. "Scrotal temperature is increased in disposable plastic lined nappies." Division of Pediatric Endocrinology, Department of Pediatrics, Christian-Albrechts-University of Kiel. May 2000.

The Cheapest Disposables vs. Cloth for Diapering Two Children

	FIRST CHILD	SECOND CHILD	TOTAL
Store-brand disposables	$900.00	$900.00	$1,800
Prefold cloth diapers, used covers, and washing expenses	$150.00 supplies $49.48 washing expenses	$49.48 washing expenses	$248.96

Assuming six thousand disposable diapers and two and a half years of washing cloth diapers per child.

Keep reading to see how we arrived at these figures.

HOW MUCH DO CLOTH DIAPER SUPPLIES COST?

You can spend anywhere from nothing (if you're lucky enough to get some hand-me-downs) to $800 on start-up costs for cloth diapering. Rebecca spent less than $150.00 on cloth diapering supplies over the two and a half years her daughter was in diapers. That cost includes three dozen prefolds and used diaper covers. If you prefer all-new pocket diapers, you may choose to buy fewer and wash them more often. If you bought two dozen bumGenius all-in-one diapers, for example, you would spend $406.80 (regular) or $529.90 (organic) for cloth diapers that your baby could wear from birth to potty training. Turn to chapter 6 for advice on choosing a cloth diapering system.

HOW MUCH DOES IT COST TO WASH AND DRY CLOTH DIAPERS?

Our best-case diaper-laundering scenario involves washing every four days in cold water with a high-efficiency machine, then hanging diapers to dry. (See chapter 6 for the logistics.) How much will washing and drying diapers cost for you? This depends on a mind-boggling list of factors, including the efficiency of your machine; the cost of water, sewer, and electricity in your area; the temperature at which you wash your laundry; and the frequency at which you wash your diapers. Using our best-case scenario, you can expect to spend on average just $.22 a load, or under $20 a year laundering your cloth diapers.

Water, Sewer, Electricity, and Detergent Usage and Costs per Year (assuming 90 loads of cloth diapers/yr)

	TOP-LOADER USAGE	TOP-LOADER COSTS	FRONT-LOADER USAGE	FRONT-LOADER COSTS
Water[7]	3,600 gallons	$9.96	1,089 gallons	$3.01
Sewer[8]	3,600 gallons	$23.04	1,089 gallons	$6.97
Electricity[9]	45 kwh (cold wash) 450 kwh (hot wash)	$4.28 (cold) $42.75 (hot)	18 kwh (cold) 180 kwh (hot)	$1.71 (cold) $17.10 (hot)
Detergent[10]	144 oz.	$12.60	90 oz.	$8.10
Total		$49.88 (cold) $88.35 (hot)		$19.79 (cold) $35.18 (hot)

A top-loader uses 40–58 gallons per load and a front-loader uses 12.1–15 gallons per load. We assumed a 40-gallon model for the top-loader and a 12.1-gallon model for the front-loader.

[7] At $2.07 per ccf, or $.002767/gallon. Check your water bill for your rate.

[8] We assumed an average rate of $4.79 per unit, or $.0064 per gallon. Sewer rates vary widely—from $1.83 per unit in Phoenix to $7.75 per unit in Seattle. Check your water/sewer bill to find your rate.

WHAT ABOUT DRYING?

If you have the time and space, it's best for your budget and the Earth to hang diapers dry. How much will you spend tumble drying diapers? A typical dryer uses 5,500 watts of electricity an hour. Assuming it takes an entire hour to dry one diaper load at $.095 a kilowatt-hour, you'd spend $.52 to dry a load of diapers, or $46.80 a year on ninety loads.

As for the environmental impact, it depends on how electricity is generated where you live. In states like Oregon, you'll release 37 pounds of carbon into the air tumble drying ninety loads of cloth diaper laundry a year. If you live in a state that relies on coal for your power (such as West Virginia, Kentucky, Wyoming, and Pennsylvania), you'll release as much as 450 pounds of carbon into the atmosphere drying your ninety cloth diaper loads. Wherever you live, the planet will thank you for hanging that laundry on a rack—even part of the time!

WHEN IS USING DISPOSABLES GREENER THAN WASHING CLOTH DIAPERS?

According to that 2005 diaper study, washing diapers in 4,000 gallons of hot water a year—and drying 20 percent of them in the dryer—is equal to using disposables and throwing them in a landfill. Take a look at your diaper-washing habits. If you have a top-loader and wash diapers in hot water every other day, you could be blowing through more than 10,000 gallons of water a year on your diaper laundry alone. If you tumble dry 180

Eco-nomical Tip

Even if you don't have time to hang diapers from the clothesline, you can offset the carbon and cost of using the dryer by air drying a load or two a week of other laundry. Sheets and towels are easy to string on clotheslines and dry quickly. If you do air dry everything, use a drying rack for those tiny baby clothes and diapers. No clothespins are required!

---

9   At $.095 per kwh, the national average. Look on your electricity bill for your rate.

10   Biokleen 10-pound box at $13.99. They recommend 1.6 ounces for top-loaders and 1 ounce for front-loaders.

101

loads of diapers a year, you could be releasing as much as 900 pounds of carbon into the air. Throw chlorine bleach in the mix and you're adding toxins to our water supply. Even with excessive washing practices, you would save money over disposables, but you probably aren't doing the planet any favors. In fact, the updated diaper study from 2008 found that it's possible to use up to 75 percent more energy if you cloth diaper inefficiently.

Don't despair, though! Take a look at our "How to Green Your Cloth Diapers" tips earlier in this chapter and see what you can do to reduce the impact of your diaper laundry habits. Washing every three days instead of every other day and hanging just one load a week will make a difference. Consider skipping bleach and using natural disinfectant such as Bac-Out by Biokleen or using a chlorine-free variety, and look into eco-friendly detergents. Keep tweaking with your system until you find something that works for you and the environment. Or, you may decide you'd rather use some of the "greener" disposables we mention later in the chapter.

Diaper Services

The Environment Agency's study concluded that the environmental impact of diaper services was about the same as the impact of washing cloth diapers at home or using disposable diapers. However, not all diaper services are the same, and many take great care in washing and transporting diapers so as to limit the detrimental effects they have on the planet. According to the National Association of Diaper Services (with the catchy acronym "NADS"!), diaper services "launder diapers to rigorous public-health standards that you couldn't possibly match at home, with thirteen changes of water and high-temperature drying that eliminates bacteria."

Go to the National Association of Diaper Services Web site, diapernet.org, to find a diaper service in your area. Call the diaper services and ask them about their washing methods, or check out their Web sites. Do they use chlorine bleach? Do they use eco-friendly detergents? How much water do they use to wash their diapers? What types of vehicles do they use to deliver the diapers? Of course, you'll also want to ask about their prices.

As an example, Tidee Didee is a diaper service that serves Portland, Oregon, as well as several cities throughout Oregon, Washington, and California. This service would deliver a fresh stack of prefold cotton diapers to your door for $13.50 to $20 a week (for 10 to 100 diapers), plus a once-a-month $5 fuel charge. This would end up costing around $1,000 a year. In addition to that, you would have to buy diaper covers, which cost anywhere from $6 to $25 new. In the first year, you'd probably need at least twelve in varying sizes.

It's apparent by looking at our diaper price charts that a diaper service would be more expensive than washing cloth diapers at home *or* using disposables—at least in our situation. However, many parents choose a diaper service as a gateway to laundering cloth diapers at home. It's also a great way to try out cloth diapering before committing to stocking up on expensive supplies. Others opt to use a service for the first few months, when everything is new and hectic, and then transition to a different system later on. Remember it's not all or nothing—you can try a service for a week, a month, or stick with it for all two and a half years of diapering your little one.

In Search of a Greener Disposable

Best Deal: **Whole Foods 365 brand chlorine-free diapers**

Best for the Planet: **gDiapers**

Best Performance and Leakage Protection: **Seventh Generation**

Best Gel-free Option: **Tushies** (the *only* gel-free option!)

There are just a handful of "greener" disposables on the market today, all of which claim to be made from chlorine-free wood pulp. Chlorine is an environmental toxin, and many parents don't want it next to baby's delicate skin. Contrary to popular belief, no green diapers available to U.S. consumers are 100 percent biodegradable, made from recycled materials, or recyclable. Even if a diaper does claim to be biodegradable, if you send it to a landfill, it cannot biodegrade. The only way to ensure that your diapers biodegrade is to home compost them—an option with gDiapers for diapers without solid waste.

You may be asking yourself if it's worth spending extra money—and all greener disposables cost more than conventional disposables—for chlorine-free diapers. If you're on a tight budget and don't want to wash cloth diapers, it may not feel like the environmental advantages of chlorine-free diapers are sufficiently compelling to warrant the higher price. One thing to consider is that many—if not all—of the companies that make chlorine-free diapers are committed to creating more sustainable products in the future. You may feel like supporting eco-conscious companies instead of mainstream companies who don't care about the planet justifies the couple hundred extra dollars you'll spend while your baby is in diapers.

THE GREENER DISPOSABLES ON THE MARKET

The most well-known green company is **Seventh Generation**, which makes a chlorine-free disposable. To date, "chlorine-free" is the only thing that distinguishes Seventh Generation from conventional brands. Seventh Generation diapers are made from chlorine-free wood pulp fluff, sodium polyacrylate (also known as SAP or absorbent gel), polyolefin nonwoven fabric, adhesives, polyolefin film, and synthetic rubber elastic strands. They do not use recycled materials in their diapers as of this writing, but they do plan to upgrade to 50 percent recycled materials in the future.

Whole Foods makes their own store-brand chlorine-free diaper. They're similar to Seventh Generation and Baby NatureCare diapers but come with a nicer price tag. If you used these diapers exclusively for your baby's six thousand diaper changes, you'd spend just $250 more than you would on Huggies.

Nature BabyCare disposable diapers are chlorine-free and claim to be 60 percent compostable. (However, we cannot see any environmental advantage of being 60 percent compostable unless you tear the diaper apart and actually compost the biodegradable components.) They do contain gel, a superabsorbent polymer (SAP). The best thing about these diapers is that even the packaging is made from "100 percent natural, renewable" material. They're available at some Target stores and online.

Tushies makes a gel-free diaper—the only gel-free disposable we've come across. Tushies are available at Whole Foods and some other specialty stores as well as online. According to their Web site, these diapers are made in the United States from "domestic materials" and "Scandinavian sustainable, renewable, family-owned forests." While it's not too green to diaper children in imported wood pulp, it's encouraging to know the origins of it, which is more than we can say about conventional disposables. Also, it's great to know that there's a gel-free disposable out there.

Finally, we have **gDiapers**, the only flushable diapers on the market. These diapers are considered a hybrid diaper. Parents buy a starter pack that comes complete with two washable cloth diaper covers. Attached to these covers is something like a little shower cap, into which you insert a disposable pad, made from tree pulp and SAP, among other things. The tree pulp comes from sustainably managed forests. Wet inserts can go into the toilet, trash, or compost bin. They're available at many grocery stores and at gdiapers. com. The fact that they're compostable gives gDiapers a huge environmental edge over the other green disposables. Is it safe to put SAP into your garden compost? According to gDiapers, SAP has been rigorously tested and deemed completely safe and nontoxic— even for human consumption! However, it is *not* biodegradable—this part of the diaper will become a part of your compost and go onto your garden. GDiapers says this is safe and points out that they actually sell SAP in nurseries. Some gardeners put it in their soil to conserve water.

Another greener component to gDiapers is the fact that solid waste—along with the gDiaper flushable liner—goes down the toilet. Most people who use disposable diapers wrap up the waste in the diaper and send it to the landfill. No matter what brand of disposable diaper you choose, you'll help the planet out by flushing solid waste down the toilet, where it can be properly managed. Where does the gDiaper go once it's in the sewer? It becomes sludge, which is sometimes converted to fertilizer. As for the SAP, it never truly goes away. Time will tell what effects—if any—SAP will have on the environment.

105

The Diapers of Tomorrow

It's important to remember that no matter what you choose to diaper your child with, it will have impact. There is really no "eco-friendly" way to diaper baby—but there are choices you can make to reduce your impact. If you choose cloth, there are many ways to make cloth diapers greener. With our tips, you can personally save thousands of dollars and almost *one ton*[11] of waste from the landfills.

Go Diaperless with Infant Potty Training

Most babies in the world don't wear diapers at all. Does this mean they just go whenever and wherever they please? No! Instead, parents pay attention to the cues their babies exhibit before elimination. Even at just a few weeks old, babies learn to wait until parents give a signal before relieving themselves.

Here in the United States, the practice is known as "elimination communication" or "infant potty training." Babies who start potty training right at birth may remain diaper free all day, although some parents still rely on a few diapers, especially when out and about. The result? Substantially fewer diapers to wash or throw away.

Linda Easton of Baby Signs, Inc., understands that infant potty training might seem overwhelming to new parents. As an alternative, she recommends waiting until the baby is a year old. With the help of infant sign language, baby can communicate when he or she has to go. "If you think that sounds too early," she says, "consider the fact that infant potty training is successfully practiced around the world and that before disposable diapers came around, 95 percent of all babies in the United States were potty trained by 18 months."

Want to learn more about infant potty training? Check out our resource section at the end of the chapter.

11 From page 47 of the diaper study, which states 3,796 used disposable diapers weigh 537.6 kg + 3 kg packaging. This results is 1,182 pounds of diaper waste per 6,000 diapers + 10.43 pounds of packaging.

If you decide to use disposables, there are several eco-minded companies you can support, whether you want a chlorine-free, gel-free, flushable, or compostable variety. These companies will look for ways to make disposables more sustainable for future generations. By the time our kids are having babies, there may very well be a diaper made from 100 percent postconsumer content that can be recycled curbside and turned into fertilizer!

Resources

- ✿ Check out the **National Association of Diaper Services** Web site, diapernet.org, to find a diaper service in your area.
- ✿ Go to **The Green Guide** (www.thegreenguide.com) and try out their laundry calculator to see how many pounds of carbon it takes you to do a load of laundry in your state.

Disposable Diaper Companies

- ✿ **gDiapers** (www.gdiapers.com) are a hybrid diaper, available at many supermarkets.
- ✿ **Nature Baby Care** (www.naty.com) can be found at some Target stores.
- ✿ **Seventh Generation** (www.seventhgeneration.com) make widely available chlorine-free disposables.
- ✿ **Tushies** (www.tushies.com) is a gel-free disposable, often found at Whole Foods.

Infant Potty Training Resources

- ✿ *Infant Potty Training: A Gentle and Primeval Method Adapted to Modern Living* by Laurie Boucke
- ✿ *Infant Potty Basics: With or Without Diapers—The Natural Way* by Laurie Boucke
- ✿ *The Diaper-Free Baby: The Natural Toilet Training Alternative* by Christine Gross-Loh
- ✿ Visit Linda Easton's Web site (www.PottyTrainWithBabySigns.com) about early potty training.

Cloth Diapering 101: Selecting and Caring for Your Cloth Diapers

Gone are the days of diaper pins and plastic pants. Today's cloth diapers are cuter, more effective, and easier to use than ever before. If you choose to eschew the disposables and jump into the world of cloth, you'll not only save hundreds of dollars but a grove of trees and several barrels of oil. You'll also keep a ton of garbage out of a landfill for each child that you swaddle in cloth.

If you are hesitant about starting cloth diapers, our best advice is to find someone who has used them to show you the ropes. Don't ask your mom or grandmother, who may have lingering memories of endless toilet-dunking and all-day laundry sagas. Cloth diapers aren't what they used to be: They don't take nearly as much time and toil as you'd think. In fact, our diaper-washing method is no more complicated than doing any other load of laundry.

If you are the only person in a hundred-mile radius considering cloth diapers, fear not. You have *The Eco-nomical Baby Guide* to lead the way. Both of us cloth diapered our babies and will divulge our insider secrets in this chapter. Before you know it, you'll be the cloth diapering expert, blazing the trail for other eco-conscious, frugal-minded parents.

Getting Started for Beginners

If you just want to try cloth diapers but don't feel like doing mounds of research and weighing all the pros and cons of each and every type, we'll help you out. The following options will get you through the first couple of months with a newborn, and after that you'll have a better idea of what will—and won't—work for you.

THE MONEY-SAVER

❀ One newborn-size pack of Seventh Generation disposable diapers (about $12)
❀ Three dozen Chinese prefolds ($36–54)
❀ Six Proraps newborn-sized diaper covers ($8.95 each new)
  Total cost: around $100

THE CUTE & CONVENIENT PACK

❀ One newborn-size pack of Seventh Generation disposable diapers (about $12)
❀ One to two dozen bumGenius 3.0 pocket cloth diapers ($180/dozen)
  Total cost: from $192–360

Other Tips for Beginners

❀ **Get a starter kit.** Many cloth diaper Web sites and diaper stores offer starter kits, which contain a variety of different diapers to try out. This is a good idea if you want to experiment with several types to see which ones work best for you and baby.

❀ **Think used.** Yes, you can buy secondhand diapers! Diaper services often sell diapers for discount prices. Keep in mind that if they're more than a dollar, you're really not saving any money over new prefolds. Consignment shops geared toward babies and kids often have great used diaper selections, allowing you to save 50 percent or more on diaper covers and pocket diapers. Plus when your child is potty trained, you can hock your used cloth diapers online at sites like Craigslist or eBay or trade them in at a resale shop for store credit—recouping some of the investment you made in cloth. We can't say the same for used disposables!

❀ **Don't buy everything at once.** It's best to buy enough cloth diapers to get you through the first few months. You can figure out what to buy next after you become a cloth diapering expert yourself. Joy was relieved that she didn't buy any infant cloth diapers when she ended up giving birth to her nine-pound son, who went right into regular prefolds and quickly moved to the next size. Rebecca was thrilled that she had only purchased the regular size when she found that her slender daughter wore them for all of her diapering years.

Prewash Your Prefolds!

Brand-new prefold diapers will be flat and nonabsorbent. You'll need to wash them a few times in hot water (with or without detergent) before using them on baby, to remove natural wax on the fibers. They'll also need to be dried in the dryer a few times to help them shrink and soften so that they will be sufficiently absorbent.

How to Put on Cloth Diapers

Many cloth diapers today are just as easy to put on as disposables. So what do we mean by, **"It goes on like a disposable"**? Before we had kids, that statement wouldn't have helped us out at all. A disposable diaper has Velcro tabs at the back that stick on to a scratchy surface on the front of the diaper and is shaped like an hourglass when laid flat so that it can be easily wrapped around baby's body. Most diaper covers, pocket diapers, and all-in-ones are designed the same way—quite an improvement over struggling to pull plastic pants on over a baby's cloth diaper!

FLAT DIAPERS

Flat diapers can be folded into thick pads and placed on a diaper cover or folded in various ways and fastened on the baby with pins or a Snappi. A cover would then go over that to protect against leaks.

PREFOLD DIAPERS

A prefold is a rectangular piece of cotton or hemp fabric that is slightly thicker through the middle section. They are called prefolds because unlike flat diapers, multiple layers of cotton are sewn together. They do require a

Step 1: Fold prefold in thirds.   Step 2: Place on diaper cover.

bit of folding before they can go in a diaper cover or on a baby. The easiest way to use a prefold is to fold it in thirds lengthwise and lay it in a diaper cover with Velcro closures. Position the baby on top of the diaper and put the diaper on the baby as you would a disposable. Some parents prefer to fasten the prefold with diaper pins or Snappis before putting on a cover. Neither of us used pins or Snappis and were happy to be able to skip this step.

POCKET DIAPERS

Pocket diapers must be stuffed with a terry insert before going on the baby. After that, they go on like disposables with snaps or Velcro closures.

ALL-IN-ONES

All in ones are shaped just like a disposable and go on just like a disposable. They are all one piece and have Velcro tabs.

113

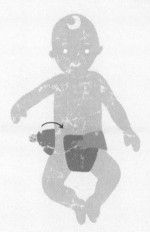

Step 3: Put baby on diaper.   Step 4: Fasten Velcro closures.

Getting Started with an Older Baby

If you are just getting started with cloth diapers but baby isn't a newborn, you can still use the advice from earlier in the chapter, except you won't need a pack of disposables, and you'll have to figure out what size diapers will fit baby. If you have a cloth diaper shop in your town, you can go in and take a look at the diapers in person and have the salespeople help you out. If you're ordering online, look at their sizing charts for the brands you're interested in. We discuss specific diaper brands and their sizes later in the chapter.

❦ **Prefolds** usually come in three sizes: infant, regular, and premium. Rebecca bought the regular size and used them from week 2 until potty training. Babies weighing less than eight pounds will fit best in the infant size. The regular size may work for babies from eight to twenty pounds. Bigger babies and heavy wetters will need the premium size.

❦ You can usually find **diaper covers** in sizes ranging from newborn, small, medium, large, and extra large. Each manufacturer will have different weight recommendations; for example, newborn size might be recommended for less than eight pounds.

❦ **Pocket diapers** come in two types. **Regular pocket diapers** such as Fuzzibunz come in a few sizes, from small to large. **Adjustable pocket diapers** such as bumGenius use a clever system of snaps so they can adjust to fit babies from seven to around thirty-five pounds.

Choosing Cloth Diapers: The Advanced Class

There are hundreds of diaper companies out there. We've tried the types we recommend and like them all. What will work best for you and your baby? You'll want to consider a few factors:

1. **How much do you want to spend?** Prefolds and covers will get the most bang for your buck—you'll save in start-up costs as well as laundry expenses. Top-of-the-line diapers include organic bumGenius diapers ($264/dozen) or organic wool options such as LANAcare (up to $50 each).

2. **How often do you want to wash diapers?** We wash diapers every four days. However, keep in mind that manufacturers recommend washing pocket diapers and all-in-ones every other day.

3. **Do you want the cloth diapers to go on easily, like a disposable?** Choose pocket diapers or all-in-ones over prefolds.

4. **Are you looking for all organic, natural fibers?** Try organic prefolds with Imse Vimse organic cotton or LANAcare wool covers. Swaddlebees makes an all-natural pocket diaper. (Most pocket diapers use synthetic material.)

5. **Which diapers offer the best protection against leaks?** We asked our readers at greenbabyguide.com which diapers offered the best leakage protection. For pocket diapers, bumGenius 3.0s do the trick, although two readers found they leaked more than other brands. Motherease diapers have a "no leaks" design many parents love. Plain old prefolds with covers were also parent favorites. (With prefolds, Rebecca liked the Imse Vimse covers the best and never had a leakage problem.)

6. **Which diapers are the best for the environment?** If the environment is your top concern when making your diaper purchases, here are our recommendations in order of eco-friendliness:

   A. **Preowned diapers.** If you buy preowned diapers and then pass them on when you're finished with them, your cloth diapers will be carbon neutral. Bonus! Secondhand diapers are also the cheapest diapering option available.

115

Comparing Cloth Diapers

DIAPER TYPE AND COST	WHAT THEY ARE	PROS	CONS
Prefolds with covers *Prefolds are $1–1.50 each. Covers cost $5–25 each.*	Several layers of absorbent cotton or hemp all sewn together with a thicker section in the middle. Fold it in thirds, place it in a diaper cover, and put it on like a disposable. A few parents prefer to pin (or Snappi) the diapers on and use nylon pants as a cover.	Least expensive diapering option, even with washing and drying You can wash as many as three dozen prefolds in one load. Dry faster than all-in-ones Made from natural materials	May seem complicated to the uninitiated When line dried, they are stiff and crunchy Require folding and placing diaper in covers
Flat diapers with covers *Flat diapers run $15 per dozen. Covers cost $5–25 each.*	One large square of thin cotton that can be folded in myriad ways. Fasten with pins or a Snappi or fold it into a thick pad and stuff it in a pocket diaper or lay it in a diaper cover.	Inexpensive diapering option Wash three dozen in a load Dry faster than any other diapers, either in the dryer or on the line Made from natural materials	May seem complicated to the uninitiated Require folding

DIAPER TYPE AND COST	WHAT THEY ARE	PROS	CONS
Pocket diapers *$15–32 each*	A fitted diaper with Velcro or snap closures and a pocket for inserting either a prefold or thick pad inside.	Easy to put on Dry faster than all-in-ones Cheaper than disposables even with washing and drying costs Line-dry more easily than prefolds Preferred by daycare providers to prefolds	More expensive than prefolds Require stuffing covers with inner layer before use Can get messy taking the inner layer out of the pocket before washing You will need to wash more frequently than prefolds because about two dozen make a full load. Most brands use man-made materials.
All-in-Ones *Around $15 each*	Made out of several layers of cotton or hemp with a water-proof outer layer. Go on like disposables with Velcro or snaps.	Easy to put on Convenient Daycares prefer them over other cloth diapers	High initial cost Take longer to dry than other diaper types Most use synthetic fabrics.

For discussion of "greener" disposable diapers, including gDiapers, see chapter 5.

B. Diapers made from organic/all natural materials. Cotton is a crop that relies on pesticides that are harmful to the environment. Organic cotton and wool options, though pricey, have a smaller footprint than other cloth diapers. Prefolds can be used as rags years after they're no longer suitable for diapers. All-natural diapers made from hemp, cotton, or wool are also biodegradable.

C. Consider that even **diapers made from man-made materials** such as bumGenius or Fuzzibunz can be used hundreds of times by more than one child, making them eco-friendlier than disposables, which are used once then tossed.

DIAPER REVIEWS

There are *hundreds* of cloth diaper types, in all shapes, sizes, and colors. We've narrowed the list down to our favorites.

- **Prefolds.** We recommend Chinese prefolds. Look for "diaper service quality." They are available in bleached or unbleached, and you may be able to find some made of organic cotton or hemp.
  Sizes: infant, regular, premium
  Cost: $1–1.50 each (Organic prefolds cost $2–3 each or more.)
- **Proraps Classic covers.** These basic covers are durable and leakproof. Be aware that they have to be air-dried or their waterproof cover will break down in the dryer over time.
  Sizes: preemie, newborn, small, medium, large, x-large
  Cost: $8.95 each

$ *Eco-nomical Tip*

Buying preowned diapers and covers will save you up to eighty percent on cloth diapering. Plus, you'll be able to resell or reuse those diapers after you're done! You'll also skip the environmental impact of growing cotton and manufacturing the diapers.

✿ **Diaperaps covers.** Another basic, inexpensive option for diaper covers. These too need to be air-dried.

Sizes: infant, newborn, small, medium, large, x-large, toddler

Cost: $9.75 each

✿ **Imse Vimse (Bumpy) diaper covers.** They make cotton ($12.50), organic cotton ($15–19), and wool diaper covers ($30).

Sizes: newborn, small, medium, large

Cost: from $12.50–30 each

✿ **bumGenius 3.0 Pocket Diapers.** These are great pocket diapers you can use from birth to potty training.

Sizes: adjust to fit babies from 7 to 35 pounds

Cost: organic bumGenius $24.95 each or $264/dozen; regular bumGenius $17.95 or $203/dozen

✿ **bumGenius all-in-one cloth diaper.** While the bumGenius 3.0 diapers adjust to fit babies from 7 to 35 pounds, they can be bulky (especially on tiny babies), so they designed this all-in-one diaper if you prefer a trimmer fit.

Sizes: x-small, small, medium, large

Cost: $15.95 each or $180/dozen

✿ **Happy Heinys adjustable pocket diapers.** This is another great adjustable pocket diaper that comes in many colorful prints.

Sizes: adjust to fit small, medium, large

Cost: $18.95 each

✿ **Fuzzibunz pocket diapers.** A popular pocket diaper with snap closures.

Sizes: x-small, small, medium, large, petite, x-large *(Note: you will probably not need every size as your baby grows; the snaps allow you to adjust the fit.)* Fuzzibunz also has a one-size diaper for $18.95 that fits babies from 7 to 35 pounds.

Cost: $17.95 each

✿ **Swaddlebees organic pocket diapers.** Organic velour pocket diapers with colorful prints and solid colors.

Sizes: small, medium, large

Cost: $18.95 each

Diaper Accessories

NECESSARY GEAR

Diaper pail – A five-gallon bucket, pail, or garbage can will hold enough for one load of diaper laundry.

Wipes – If you chose to use cloth wipes instead of disposables, buy them when you purchase your cloth diapers or make them yourself out of a flannel blanket or cotton T-shirts.

Diaper wet bag – If you want to use cloth diapers at daycare, on the go, or on trips, you'll need a bag to store your wet or soiled diapers. We recommend Monkey Foot Designs wet bags if you want to be stylish, a rafting dry bag from a sporting-goods store if you want to be practical, and a zippered plastic bag if you want to be economical.

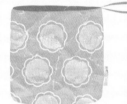

OPTIONAL (OR EVEN PLAIN UNNECESSARY) GEAR

Wipe warmer – If you use homemade wipes, you may want to keep them in a wipe warmer. Of course it's *much* greener to just keep your wipes stacked and wet them with a spray or squirt bottle when needed. Use plain water.

120

Snappi – A Snappi is an alternative to diaper pins, used to fasten a prefold on a baby before the diaper cover goes on. (Neither of us needed these with prefold diapers. We just put them in the cover and fastened them on with Velcro.)

Diaper pins – Some parents still prefer old-fashioned diapering methods, and use pins to secure a flat or prefold diaper on the baby. There's no reason you'll need these if you decide to go with Velcro covers, pocket diapers, or all-in-ones.

Diaper sprayer – You can affix a special sprayer to the toilet and use it to spray off diapers. Hold off on this purchase until you're sure it's necessary. We survived by just dunking our soiled diapers in the toilet without incident.

Diaper liners – Once the baby is eating solid foods, you'll need to make sure solid waste goes in the toilet. Flushable diaper liners make this step much easier for cloth-diapering parents. You may not need them, however. Not to get too graphic, but some babies' waste plops off the diaper and into the toilet without creating a mess.

121

Using Cloth Diapers at Night

Is it possible to use cloth diapers overnight? Of course! Until about thirty years ago, everyone relied on cloth full time. In the beginning, your nighttime diaper may not be any different from a daytime diaper, but as baby sleeps longer and longer, you'll find yourself needing a more absorbent solution. Here are some tips:

- If you use prefolds, double them up and use a bigger diaper cover at night.

- If you use pocket diapers, try stuffing them with extra inserts.

- Invest in diaper doublers, which are essentially extra pads to stick under a prefold or in a pocket diaper.

- Try woolen covers, which will help wick away the moisture better than other materials.

- Use pocket diapers such as Fuzzibunz or bumGenius to help keep baby's skin dry at night. Some parents love this, whereas others have found that the synthetic material contributes to diaper rashes.

Washing Your Cloth Diapers

In chapter 5 we presented a "best-case scenario" for washing diapers. If you really want to do what's best for the environment, you will collect your diapers in a dry pail, wash them in cold water, and hang them dry. However, we know that the "best-case scenario" isn't always possible. We found that we were able to treat a load of diapers like any other load of laundry: We washed in cold water on the heavy cycle, then dried them in the dryer. We recommend starting with a minimalist approach and adding extra rinses or hotter water only if necessary.

THE TEN-MINUTE METHOD

This method takes six minutes of hands-on work every time you wash a batch of diapers. If you wash diapers every four days, that amounts to about ten minutes of diaper-related work a week.

We don't count the time it takes to change the diaper, because since we don't use pins or Snappis, changing takes no more time with a cloth diaper than with a disposable. We also do not consider the time it may take to dump (and possibly dunk) the diaper in the toilet to get rid of "solid deposits," as disposable-users should be doing this for the sake of the environment as well. Believe it or not, disposable diaper boxes all include a recommendation to dump solid waste before tossing in the trash.

Keep in mind that this "ten-minute method" applies to people who have washers and dryers at home. Rebecca's machine is in the basement, so the times include running up and down the stairs. Your results may vary!

Step One (2 minutes): Carry bucket of diapers to machine, put in machine with detergent, adjust settings to heavy cycle/cold water, press the start button. Return empty bucket, wash hands.

Step Two (1 minute): Run to basement, put clean diapers in dryer, return upstairs, spread out wraps to dry.

Step Three (3 minutes): Retrieve dry diapers and wipes, stack them, and put them away.

Tips for the Lazy and Nonchalant

❦ **Don't run an extra rinse cycle.** Try running a heavy cycle first. If that doesn't do the trick, add more cycles later. Joy was running two cycles until Rebecca asked her, "Why?" She stopped the extra rinse cycle and noticed no difference in the cleanliness of her diapers.

❦ **Don't use a wet pail or rinse diapers.** Just throw them in the bucket. That is how they do it if you use a diaper service. Using a dry pail saves water and keeps the diaper pail lighter. Plus the "diaper soup" that brews when diapers sit in a wet pail is both disgusting and time consuming. Start messing with wet pails and deodorizers only if you are having problems with the "slacker method."

❧ **Gross tidbit ahead:** While your baby eats just breast milk or formula, diapers can go straight to the pail. Formula-fed diapers will produce more "aromatic" waste however, which may cause you to consider more frequent washings or flushable liners. After introducing solids, waste should go in the toilet and be dealt with by the sewer system instead of being thrown into our landfills. If you are lucky, once your baby is eating solid foods he will produce deposits that simply fall off the diaper and into the toilet. If you are unlucky, you may have to subject yourself to the dreaded "toilet dunk." In that case you may find yourself looking into diaper liners or gadgets (such as the Toilet Duck) designed to assist you in rinsing the diapers before they hit the pail.

❧ **Don't use pins or Snappis.** If you use all-in-one diapers, this is a nonissue. But even prefolds can be folded in thirds and placed in a diaper cover without being pinned.

❧ **Don't fold anything.** Joy folds her diapers in thirds so they are ready for diaper changes, but Rebecca just stacks hers. There is the even lazier method, of throwing all the clean diapers in a drawer or basket. Voilà! This probably shaves a good three minutes off our ten-minute plan.

See chapter 8 for cloth diaper tips for apartment dwellers.

Frequently Asked Questions about Washing and Drying Diapers

Q: How often do I need to wash cloth diapers?

A: It depends. We suggest buying enough diapers to wash a full load every four days. Pocket diaper manufacturers recommend washing every other day.

Q: What is the difference between a wet pail and a dry pail?

A: Some people like to soak their diapers in water before washing them, sometimes with a little bleach, baking soda, or detergent. That is a wet pail. With a dry pail, you simply toss the diapers in the bucket and leave them there until washing day. We prefer the dry pail method.

Q: How many diapers do I wash at once?

A: Three dozen prefolds or two dozen pocket diapers can be washed in most standard-size washing machines. Do not overload your machine, or your diapers may not get clean.

Q: What special detergents or chemicals do I need to wash my diapers?

A: We like Biokleen laundry powder for its effectiveness and reasonable price. (In fact, wash per wash it actually comes out costing less than mainstream generic brands of detergent.) If desired, use white vinegar in the rinse cycle to avoid detergent buildup, disinfect, and deodorize.

Q: Is it sanitary to wash diapers in cold water?

A: Cold water does not sanitize cloth diapers—but neither does hot water, unless it is boiling. If your washer has a sanitary cycle, the water *will* get hot enough to disinfect. Try starting with the method that uses the least amount of water and energy first. You use three types of energy to wash laundry: thermal energy (from the water temperature), mechanical energy (from your washing machine's action), and chemical energy (from the detergents and other chemicals you add to the laundry). If your diapers aren't getting clean enough, you can experiment with water temperature, cycle times, and detergent amounts.

Q: My diapers are stained! What do I do?

A: Sunlight is the best way to get rid of diaper stains. Just set out diapers—either wet or dry—in the sun and stains will disappear in hours. Several diaper manufacturers recommend using hydrogen peroxide to whiten diapers. You can also try using Biokleen's Bac-Out as an alternative to chlorine bleach.

Q: What products are not recommended for washing diapers?

A: Avoid detergents with phosphates or chlorine, both of which are harmful to the environment. Also avoid products with optical brighteners. Heavily scented detergents—both artificial and natural—can coat your diapers with oils and cause unpleasant smells.

125

Smelly Diaper Trouble-Shooting

You're dutifully laundering your diapers according to our directions, and yet when you pull them from the washer they smell horrible. What could be the problem? The following list includes a few possible culprits.

DETERGENT BUILDUP. Residue from detergent including fragrances or oils can build up in fibers and cause them to hold onto smells and become less absorbent. If this happens to your diapers, wash previously laundered diapers in hot water and a hot rinse without any type of laundry detergent. You can run the rinse a few times to make sure the buildup is gone. Also, be sure that you aren't adding too much detergent to your loads so that buildup doesn't become a frequent issue. You'll only need about half as much for diaper laundry as you use for clothing.

THE WRONG DETERGENT. Certain brands contain too much washing soda that can cause problems for people with very hard water. Some parents have complained that Arm & Hammer detergents can cause problems with laundering diapers in hard water.

VINEGAR. Depending on the hardness or softness of your water, vinegar will be either helpful or harmful. If you're using vinegar and the smell continues, try switching to hydrogen peroxide, baking soda or Bac-Out (an enzyme based odor eliminator made by Biokleen). If you're struggling with smelly diapers and haven't tried vinegar yet, add about a third of a cup to your diaper laundry and see if it makes a difference.

SYNTHETIC FABRIC. We've found that polyester hangs onto smells much more than cotton. You may need to launder synthetic diapers more frequently and/or add hydrogen peroxide on a regular basis. Manufacturers of polyester diapers recommend hydrogen peroxide because it neutralizes the acidity of urine.

IMPROPER LOADING. Are you possibly overfilling the washer? Experiment with load size and see if it makes a difference.

Q: Should I add bleach to each load of cloth diapers?

A: No. Diaper manufacturers recommend against using bleach because it can damage the fibers and contribute to wear and tear on your diapers. In addition, chlorine bleach is an environmental toxin. For gentler stain removal techniques, keep reading.

Q: I tried drying my prefold cloth diapers on the clothesline and they ended up as stiff as boards. Should I go back to tumble drying them?

A: Tumble drying is the only way to get prefolds soft and fluffy. However, we've found that line-dried prefolds will soften up considerably when tossed in the dryer with another load of laundry. If you never use a dryer at all, it may be best to use another type of cloth diaper such as pocket diapers, which maintain a soft surface when air-dried.

Q: I hung my diapers on a rack in my house and it took more than a week before they were dry. Obviously this is not practical. Should I give up on line-drying my diapers?

A: Any amount of line drying will cut down on the time clothes need in the dryer—and reduce your carbon emissions. You could try drying diapers on a line overnight and then tossing in the dryer to finish the job the next day.

Q: My diapers seem smelly, even right from the wash. What can I do?

A: Smelly diapers could be caused by detergent buildup. To strip them, wash them a few times in hot water with no detergent and use white vinegar in the rinse cycle. If you use white vinegar every time you wash diapers, this may prevent any buildup in the first place. Also make sure you are not using too much detergent. Use about half of what you'd use on a normal load of laundry. Setting your diapers out in the sunshine will also get rid of unpleasant diaper odors.

Q: My child is getting diaper rashes and yeast infections. Is this because of the cloth diaper?

A: Maybe. Some parents claim disposables cause rashes, others find that cloth diapers are the culprits. To treat the rash, consult with your baby's pediatrician. As for your cloth diapers, we have a few ideas:

127

❡ If your baby gets yeast infections, first wash your diapers in 122° Fahrenheit water (you may have to turn your water heater up temporarily) to kill all yeast. Using vinegar in the rinse cycle, drying diapers in the dryer, and hanging them in sunlight will also kill yeast. Also, increase the frequency of diaper changes. Some parents have trouble with yeast when using a cloth diaper at night but have no trouble with it during the day. If that's the case, try that extra hot rinse to kill the yeast. After that you can resume your normal methods.

❡ Are your diapers made from synthetic or natural materials? Synthetic materials may cause a too-warm environment that encourages yeast growth. Try using cotton or wool diapers, at least next to baby's skin. On the other hand, some parents find the fleece on pocket diapers such as Fuzzibunz helps wick away moisture, *preventing* diaper rashes!

❡ Apply diaper cream before putting on the evening diaper. It will provide a barrier against wetness.

Using Hydrogen Peroxide for Nonchlorine Bleach

If you'd like your diapers to be clean and odor free without chlorine bleach, we have just the solution for you. It turns out that those bottles of chlorine-free bleach are filled with 3 percent hydrogen peroxide mixed with water—which is exactly what you'll get by buying hydrogen peroxide at the drugstore. It is cheaper and will provide you with the same nonchlorine bleach.

FOR THE WASH: Add ¼ cup of hydrogen peroxide to each wash load, or a bit more for very full or dirty loads.

FOR STAINS: Douse them with hydrogen peroxide and then spot wash with detergent. It's best not to let the hydrogen peroxide sit on the fabric for a long period of time.

FOR HOUSEHOLD USE: Just add ½ cup hydrogen peroxide to one gallon of water and use on the kitchen sink, tile, bathroom, shower, toilet, and bathtub.

Tossing hydrogen peroxide into a load of dirty diapers will make a big difference in smell. It neutralizes the acidity, which is the cause of the smell. While some people have found that vinegar works, it can exacerbate the problem depending on the chemistry of the water in your area since it's also highly acidic.

Offsetting the Water and Energy Used to Wash and Dry Your Diapers

You may wonder if all the water and energy used to wash cloth diapers makes them any better for the planet than disposables—a topic we discuss in detail in the previous chapter. If you worry about wasting resources, here are a few ideas to help you offset the water and energy you'll use washing and drying those diapers.

- ❧ First of all, make sure you're not wasting water with unnecessary soaking and rinsing.

- ❧ Look into getting a high-efficiency washer. You may find with all the tax credits you'll get for switching to a front-loader that it's much more affordable than you imagine. Rebecca was prepared to spend $800 on a front-loading washer before her daughter was born and walked away with a $350 machine due to a sale and tax credits!

- ❧ The dryer releases up to 5 pounds of carbon into the air every time you run a load. (See chapter 5 for more details.) Try hanging dry a load of laundry every week to offset the time your diapers spend in the dryer.

- ❧ Remember that once your child is potty-trained, he or she will be using more water with toilet flushes than you did on extra diaper laundry. (Each time you flush you use between 1.6 and 3 gallons of water depending on the efficiency of your toilet. If your child uses the bathroom six times per day, you'll flush between 9.6 and 18 gallons daily!)

The Thrill of Cloth

After a few months of examining cloth diapers online, trying them on your baby, and dutifully washing them, you notice something a bit peculiar: You actually *enjoy* using them. You find yourself browsing Web sites for new cloth diaper styles, admiring your diapers flapping on the clothesline, and extolling the merits of pocket diapers . . . to your child-free friends. You don't just put up with cloth diapers because you want to save a few bucks or out of a devotion to the planet—you actively *like* cloth diapering. When you strike up a conversation with a total stranger over the softness of the new bumGenius liners, you'll know that you have truly reached cloth-diapering nirvana. It happened to us; we hope it happens for you, too.

Resources

Don't forget to look for local diaper shops. Nothing beats visiting a diaper store in person to look at all the available styles. Plus, you'll be able to talk to the shopkeepers who probably know a thing or two about cloth diapering.

Diaper Companies

The companies below sell their own diapers. Their Web sites are also great places to find tips on washing diapers, weigh-ins on the environmental debate, and disposable vs. cloth cost-comparison analyses.

- **Diaperaps** (www.diaperaps.com) offers basic diaper covers to go over prefolds. You can also get diaper liners through this company.

- **Cottonbabies** (www.cottonbabies.com) is the company that brings BumGenius diapers, which are adjustable diapers that can fit your baby from birth to potty-training. Cottonbabies also sells prefolds and an all-in-one.

- **Happy Heinys** (www.happyheinys.com) also has adjustable pocket diapers with great prints.

- ✿ **Fuzzibunz** (www.fuzzibunz.com) is a very popular pocket diaper.

- ✿ **Mother-ease** (www.mother-ease.com) has a leak-free system and offers one adjustable diaper style that can be paired with a waterproof cover.

Online Stores

You can go through the brands directly, or buy via an online store. Here are a few online diaper stores to check out:

- ✿ **Abbys Lane** (www.abbyslane.com) carries Swaddlebees organic diapers.

- ✿ **Baby Bunz & Co.** (www.babybunz.com)

- ✿ **Baby Naturale** (www.babynaturale.com)

- ✿ **Better for Babies** (www.betterforbabies.com)

- ✿ **Cottontail Baby** (www.cottontailbaby.com)

- ✿ **Diaper Junction** (www.diaperjunction.com)

- ✿ **Eco Baby** (www.ecobaby.com)

- ✿ **Green Mountain Diapers** (www.greenmountaindiapers.com) carries LANAcare wool diapers and Imse Vimse wool covers.

- ✿ **My Baby First** (www.mybabyfirst.com)

- ✿ And of course, **The Green Baby Guide** (www.greenbabyguide.com) has dozens of diaper posts from us, diaper brand reviews, diaper style debates, and tips from our readers.

7

Into the Mouths of Babes: Practical Ways to Feed Your Baby and Save the World

Modern baby-feeding seems to require hundreds of baby food jars, dozens of plastic bottles, and lots of commercially grown food. Is it possible to minimize the gear, buy organic, and save yourself a few hundred dollars? It's not only possible, but far easier than you can imagine. In this chapter you'll find plenty of resources for breastfeeding, comparisons of organic formulas, and tips for a healthy transition to solid food.

Breastfeeding: Use Milk-Making Superpowers to Save the Planet (and some cash)

Forgive us. We're about to launch into all the reasons why breastfeeding is the very best option available to new moms. If you absolutely can't breastfeed for any reason, please don't read this. We don't want to cause undue guilt just because breastfeeding isn't possible. Skip to the next section on organic formulas if this applies to you. If you're on the fence, however, you'll want to know about why breastfeeding is such a healthy choice for you, baby, and the planet.

The Top Ten Reasons to Breastfeed

1. **Nutrition.** Unlike formula, which is derived from the milk of other animals or synthesized from plant proteins, breast milk is specially formulated to meet all of your child's nutritional needs. It also naturally evolves to include the nutrients that baby requires at different developmental stages.

2. **Baby's health.** If you breastfeed baby you'll pass along the antibodies you've gained from inoculations and sicknesses. (The immunity won't last once you stop providing breast milk, however.) In addition, studies have found that breastfed babies have far fewer risks associated with a wide variety of illnesses including asthma, obesity, childhood leukemia, and SIDS. Babies who are not breastfed have a whopping 21 percent higher mortality rate than their breastfed counterparts.

3. **Mother's health.** Breastfeeding uses up extra calories that help mothers shed pregnancy pounds. In addition it helps the uterus shrink back to its original size and may minimize a woman's bleeding after giving birth. Breastfeeding also lowers a woman's risk for ovarian and breast cancer.

4. **Eco-friendliness.** Instead of having to toss out several dozen formula containers and wash a few hundred bottles over the course of the first six months, breastfeeding requires nothing but you and baby. Even if you pump, you'll wash far fewer bottles and have much less planetary impact than if you feed your child formula. This is especially true when you take into account the energy needed to manufacture formula, package it up, and ship it all around the country.

5. **Cost savings**. Organic formula will cost upward of $8,000 for baby's first year. Beyond that expense, studies show that medical costs of exclusively formula-fed babies tend to be higher since they have more illnesses including ear infections, diarrhea, and respiratory illnesses. If you breastfeed full time you'll have to eat a few hundred more calories a day, but otherwise it's virtually free.

6. **Bonding.** Breastfeeding entails plenty of skin-to-skin contact, which is good for your child's development and the maternal connection. Plus, it forces you to sit down, put your feet up, and gaze into your newborn's eyes at regular intervals.

7. **Comfort.** When baby is sick, hurting, or distraught, breastfeeding provides a natural soothing effect. It's empowering to know that as a mother you have the ability to ease your child's pain in an instant.

8. **Brain development.** A study published in the *American Journal of Clinical Nutrition* showed that breastfed infants had a 5.2-point advantage in IQ tests. The study looked at more than seven thousand children. The author of the study believes that 40 percent of that advantage is due to the increased maternal bonding between infant and child and that 60 percent of the increase is due to the nutritional value of breast milk.

9. **Convenience.** Breastfeeding families don't have to schlep cans of formula around or warm up bottles in the middle of the night. Being with baby is all you need to be able to provide instant nourishment.

10. **Other Mysterious Benefits.** Cathatrina Svanborg, a physician and immunologist at Lund University in Sweden, was searching for a way to fight germs when she mixed cancer cells with a few drops of breast milk. Surprisingly, she found that one of the components of breast milk compels all sorts of cancer cells to die. In fact, every type of cancer cell they tested was killed when exposed to breast milk. While scientists don't yet fully understand the implications of the study, it does show that breast milk might have benefits that we haven't yet discovered.

Eating Well during Pregnancy and Breastfeeding

If you have the option of ingesting only organic food during this critical time, go for it! If you're trying to balance budgetary concerns with environmental ideals, pick organic items at the top of the food chain first. Organic meats, dairy, and eggs all are very closely regulated. If you can only afford some organic items, start there and carefully wash your mainstream produce before consumption. Also, consider the pesticide chart later in the chapter to decide which produce items need to be organic and which mainstream fruits and veggies have lower pesticide residue.

The following snacks have kept pregnant moms happily satisfied while providing quality nutrition.

- Almonds
- Unsulphured dried apricots
- Peanut butter on multigrain toast
- Whole-grain cereal
- Homemade hot chocolate or steamed milk
- Pita or veggies dipped in hummus
- Full-fat yogurt with fruit
- Sliced mango in lime juice
- Avocado drizzled with sweet wine vinegar

Donating Breast Milk through a Milk Bank

If you end up with more breast milk than you need, premature babies, ill babies, or newborns with extreme allergies can benefit from your milk. With a prescription in hand from a pediatrician, families can purchase breast milk from one of eleven milk banks in North America. The donors are prescreened, and the milk is pasteurized to ensure that supplies are safe for all the recipients. You can contact WakeMed Mother's Milk Bank or the Human Milk Banking Association of North America to donate your milk. A baby across the country could benefit immensely from the breast milk that you would otherwise toss down the drain.

How Long Should You Breastfeed?

In those first few days and weeks of breastfeeding, it can be hard to imagine keeping it up for another day, let alone the entire year recommended by the American Academy of Pediatrics. The good news is that you don't really need to make the decision either way until you've gotten the hang of breastfeeding and parenting. Even then, baby might make the decision for you by deciding to wean a bit earlier than anticipated. Whatever happens, remember that any amount of breastfeeding is beneficial to baby, and it's up to you and your child to decide how long to continue.

When Joy was still pumping at work and crawling out of bed for nighttime feedings, she clung to the dream of weaning at one year. However when her son was hospitalized with a febrile seizure right around his first birthday, she found that breastfeeding helped him through the painful medical tests he had to endure. It was such a comfort for her to be able to provide nourishment and support for her son that she ended up breastfeeding just a few times a day for another eight months. Her son slowly lost interest in breastfeeding when he was about twenty months old and weaned easily.

Rebecca, on the other hand, was thrilled that her daughter self-weaned at thirteen months. She found it freeing to leave the sitter with a cup of milk for Audrey rather than

137

having to worry about pumping or breastfeeding. While she's glad she did breastfeed for the first year, she had no desire to continue beyond that time span.

Every extra month that you do breastfeed has environmental benefits. Breastfeeding eliminates the need to drive to the store, purchase a product that has to be manufactured and packaged, and dispose of the container. Even if you buy organic milk or formula, dairy farms have a tremendous environmental impact just because of the animal waste produced and the land occupied by the animals. Opting to breastfeed instead is far more environmentally beneficial.

Our recommendation is that you make the decision for your baby when the time comes based on your own feelings and your baby, rather than societal pressures. There's no reason that a walking, talking child shouldn't be breastfeeding. The World Health Organization recommends breastfeeding for at least two years, as does the United Nations Children's Fund (UNICEF). If you would like support for your extended breastfeeding efforts, go to La Leche League's Web site or read Dr. William Sears' *The Baby Book* to find more information.

Storing Breast Milk

Joy went back to work part time just six weeks after her baby was born and found that she had to pump and store milk at least once during the day in her staff fridge. Co-workers were pretty tolerant of her breast milk containers being shoved into the top shelf among lunches and snacks. She added a session of pumping in the evenings and always had plenty of milk available for her daycare provider. (For more pumping at work stories, flip to chapter 8.)

While some moms have to bring several prepared bottles for childcare, Joy brought just one bottle to daycare each day. She froze one-ounce cubes of milk and transported them in freezer bags so that her son always had a backup supply. Her provider could pop a few ice cubes in a bottle and defrost it in a container of hot water, so no precious milk was wasted. Silicone ice trays are a better bet than the plastic varieties since they're BPA-free, but you can also purchase a product specifically designed for freezing breast milk. See the resource section at the end of the chapter for more details.

Troubleshooting Breastfeeding Challenges

While breastfeeding is ideal, it isn't always easy in the first few weeks. Still, it's worth the early investment of time and energy to be able to breastfeed with ease in the months to come. Check the resource guide at the end of the chapter for some great online breastfeeding support.

"The first 3 weeks of breastfeeding my first were the hardest learning curve I've had to cope with . . . but once we had it sorted, it worked like a dream. SO convenient to be able to feed your baby anywhere, anytime. My kids have been fed in some unusual places—beside a waterfall, on the beach, in the park . . ."

PENNY DUGMORE, Auckland, New Zealand

"My little man is six months old, and breastfeeding is more of a challenge, or maybe I should say more of a commitment, than I had imagined. Especially since my son is pretty antibottle, which means I can never leave him for very long. But I do find some satisfaction in knowing that I can comfort him in a way nobody else can. My favorite thing right now is the way he plays with my hair, necklace, shirt, etc. while he nurses. And then he'll often pull off midfeed and smile SO big at me, and then latch back on and keep eating. I love it! So worth it!"

AMY WATSON, Spring Hill, Tennessee

"I lost weight in a ridiculous amount of time, get to hug her for hours a day, and know that I am giving her the absolute best start possible. Remember in the wee hours that the first month is only a month, but the benefits last a lifetime."

EMILY IVEY, Bay Minette, Alabama

We highly recommend perseverance in those early days of breastfeeding, but realize that some women aren't able to continue because of postpartum depression or other medical issues. Be prepared to let go of your breastfeeding dreams if you've pursued every possible avenue for finding breastfeeding support. It won't mean you are a less than perfect parent! Also remember that it isn't all or nothing. You can breastfeed for a month and decide to switch to formula later, or you can choose to supplement breastfeeding with bottle feeding. It's important to find a system that works for baby and you.

Organic Formulas: Worth the Price?

A decade ago there was just one American company making organic formula, but that trend is rapidly changing. Organic formula sales made a nearly tenfold growth between 2005 and 2007, and manufacturers are rushing to meet the demands of a growing market share.

Why choose organic? Organic formulas don't contain hormones or pesticides that could be detrimental to a baby's health. From an environmental standpoint, organic formula is preferable because it's made without polluting our air and water supplies.

How can I know that a formula is actually organic? Look for the USDA Organic seal on the package, which signifies that 95 percent of the product's ingredients must be grown without the use of certain pesticides and herbicides. The milk-based formulas must come from cows that aren't given growth hormones, antibiotics, or other chemicals.

Are all organic formulas equal? Many aspects of organic formula are similar, but there are a few ingredients that need to be carefully examined. For example, Similac Organic Formula includes sucrose, a type of sugar that is cheaper than cow's milk-derived lactose but is widely considered to be ultrasweet. Since Similac formula tastes so much sweeter to babies (which has been verified in tests by adults as well), it may lead babies to refuse to switch formulas or resist foods without the sugary taste to which they've become accustomed. Babies Only uses brown rice syrup, which is generally considered to be superior even to lactose as a natural sweetener.

How much more will organic formula cost? On average, organic formula will cost 30 percent more than traditional formula, but there are ways to cut the costs by buying in bulk. Going organic can stretch the budget, but you can potentially offset the cost of buying organic by using other cost-cutting measures, such as cloth diapering or outfitting your nursery with used gear.

Should I worry about using regular tap water to mix with formula? If you'd prefer to use a filtration system, that's fine, but we recommend against using bottled water. Plastic water bottles can leach toxins over time, and the environmental cost of bottled water is just too great, especially considering that the industry doesn't have a certification system for ensuring that bottled water is better than what comes out of your faucet.

Should I look for an organic formula containing ARA, an omega-3 fatty acid, and DHA, an omega-6 fatty acid? Not necessarily. Those ingredients are derived from algae and fungus, which are sometimes treated with harsh chemicals. There are concerns that the overprocessing of these compounds might counteract their health benefits. For more information on ARA and DHA, go to the Cornucopia Institute Web page, www.cornucopia.org.

Should I buy powdered or premade? In tests conducted by the Environmental Working Group, premade infant formula had some of the highest BPA levels of any canned food. (BPA, also known as Biphesonal-A, is a chemical that mimics estrogen and has been linked to several types of cancer and other diseases in laboratory rats.) In addition to the health concerns, premade formula is both economically and environmentally wasteful. Powdered formula is definitely the best option.

What brands do you recommend? In the chart on the following page we've compared the organic formula brands on the market. It's important to note that brands will be emerging after this book is published that are not included in our information. Check online to see if there are more current options available to you today.

Our favorite is Baby's Only by Nature's One. Although it states that it can only be used as a toddler formula after one year of age, the company mainly wants to ensure that parents breastfeed for the first year. If breastfeeding isn't an option, Baby's Only compares well with every other infant formula, but you can check with your pediatrician first to ensure it's appropriate.

141

$ *Eco-nomical Tip*

Not only will breastfeeding save you thousands of dollars compared to the cost of formula, you'll also be feeding baby ultranutritious food without leaving a carbon footprint. Breastfeeding requires no production, packaging, transportation, or disposal.

Organic Formulas: How Do They Compare?

BRAND	VARIETIES	CONTAIN ARA AND DHA	SWEETENERS	AVERAGE PRICE PER OUNCE
Baby's Only by Nature's One	Soy, Dairy, Lactose-Free	No	Brown Rice Syrup	$.71
Bright Beginnings	Dairy	Yes	Lactose	$.97
Earth's Best	Dairy and Soy	Yes	Lactose	$1.13
Parent's Choice/ Member's Mark (generic version of Earth's Best available only at WalMart)	Dairy and Soy	Yes	Lactose	$.58
Similac Organic	Dairy	Yes	Sucrose	$1.17

Transitioning to Solid Foods

For many families, the transition to solid foods entails a trip to the grocery store to pick out a few multicolored bottles of puree. While there are several varieties of organic baby foods on store shelves, you can also easily concoct your own baby food for a fraction of the environmental and economic cost. With some organic produce and a few appliances you already own, you'll be well on your way to feeding baby healthy, home-prepared meals for just pennies.

Controlling the Cost of Organic Food

What if you can't afford to buy *everything* organic? You can try to at least avoid or carefully wash the foods with the highest pesticide levels. Below is a list of the best bets for low pesticide residue in conventional foods as well as the fruits and veggies with the highest levels of residue. (Courtesy of the Environmental Working Group.) According to a simulation by the EWG, people can cut their pesticide exposure by 90 percent just by avoiding the foods with the highest residues!

Highest Pesticide Residue	Lowest Pesticide Residue
Peaches	Onions
Apples	Avocados
Sweet Bell Peppers	Sweet Corn (Frozen)
Celery	Pineapples
Cherries	Mangoes
Lettuce	Sweet Peas (Frozen)
Grapes (Imported from Chile)	Asparagus
Pears	Kiwis
Spinach	Bananas
Potatoes	Cabbage
Nectarines	Broccoli
Strawberries	Eggplant

Items higher up the food chain like dairy and meats can potentially contain higher levels of toxins. Eating organic meat and dairy products is an eco-friendly way to ensure your food is good for you, and if you can find local organic products, that's even better. Even if you can't afford all organic products all the time, buying them whenever possible still benefits your health and the planet.

143

Only the Best for Baby: Organic First Foods

Believe it or not, *Consumer Reports*, the ultimate thrifty guide, recommends spending a bit extra on organic baby food not just for the sake of the environment, but for baby's health. Even if you cannot afford to continue feeding your children organic produce throughout their lifetime, doing it when they are infants has the most impact since their developing body is tiny and more vulnerable to toxins than it will be later in life. We'll show you how to cut the cost of organic foods by making them yourself and compare the cost of jarred foods on the market. Look on the following pages for organic baby food recipes you can blend up in the comfort of your kitchen.

Baby's First Foods

What about that first meal? It's important to check with your pediatrician, but you'll most likely hear that baby can be given iron-enriched cereal mixed with breast milk or formula. The other school of thought involves skipping the baby cereal altogether and jumping right into whole foods, such as bananas or sweet potatoes. Rebecca's daughter Audrey's first food was avocado!

If you want to make your own baby gruel, try pureeing well-cooked rice with hot water and a bit of breast milk. You can make oat cereal out of oat bran and hot water, too. Rebecca bought organic oats for $.99 a pound, ground them with her food processor, and made that into a porridge for her daughter. (You can get a liquid vitamin supplement from your doctor if you want to enrich baby's diet with iron and other nutrients.) For months Audrey would eat *anything* as long as it was added to her oats—even kale, black beans, and broccoli.

Aside from feeling better about giving her daughter organic whole grains instead of conventional single-grain cereal that contains preservatives, she saved money. Organic oats run around $1 to $2 a pound, whereas one 8-ounce box of Gerber single-grain rice cereal costs $2.50—or $5 a pound!

Green Moms' Perspectives on Baby's First Meal

"I found people to be seriously obsessed with the idea of rice cereal as a first food! It was crazy how they just insisted it was what baby must eat. Instead we gave her baked sweet potato in chunks and let her feed herself. She continues to love eating and does a great job deciding how much and of what foods she will eat."

JEN M., Arlington, Massachusetts

"Her first mushy cereal was actually a desire to try my usual breakfast oatmeal. Off and on she liked it, and I experimented with what went in it. Now, like me, she eats a variety of hot whole grains for breakfast and a variety of grains, beans, and veg during the day. As a toddler, we are extended breastfeeders, but she eats mostly real food (as opposed to 'baby' food) during the day.

"There is also some thought out there that we do not necessarily make the new foods mushy, which is a turn-off to some babies. Instead, to avoid a choking hazard and to include a variety of textures, there are a number of mesh baggies that allow the children to sort of gnaw on things as they develop desires for them."

BEV DIAZ, Lansdowne, Pennsylvania

(Authors' note: The mesh bags she's referring to are found in most baby food sections of major grocery stores. Fresh fruit or veggies are popped into the mesh bag attached to a plastic handle so that kids can safely gnaw at them without risk of choking.)

How We Went Organic without Breaking the Bank

"When my daughter turned six months old, I signed up for an organic veggie delivery. Every two weeks I had about fifteen pounds of seasonal, local vegetables delivered for $30. While this cost more than the very cheapest vegetables at the supermarket, I was able to feed my daughter 100 percent homemade, organic food in her first year for a fraction of the cost of jarred baby food."

REBECCA

"I returned to work determined to do everything in the cheapest, most eco-friendly way possible, including making all our baby food from scratch. After six months of sleep deprivation, we decided to compromise and embrace those tiny jars of freedom. We did blend up sweet potatoes and avocado and freeze them in cubes for our son, but we also bought large containers of non-baby foods like organic pumpkin, applesauce, and squash. When we did need jarred foods, we bought Earth's Best foods in large quantities from Costco and found it to be just a few cents more per jar than mainstream baby food."

JOY

Making Your Baby Food from Scratch

All you truly need to get started is some organic produce; a blender, food processor, immersion blender, potato masher, or food mill; and a few ice cube trays. (Again, you'll want to use silicone trays or pick some specifically designed for baby that are listed at the end of the chapter in the resource section.) Simply peel and boil, bake, or steam the food, blend it with some extra water until it reaches the desired texture, and pour it into ice cube trays. Food for younger babies should be smooth and soft enough to ensure there's no choking hazard. As babies age you can blend the food less and less to provide more texture. There's no need for salt or sugar but you can add seasonings as long as they're not too spicy.

To store your ice cubes, dump them into freezer bags with labels and dates. It's convenient to prepare large batches, but it can backfire when your child rejects sweet potatoes after you've made several dozen servings. Still, babies need to experiment with new tastes several times before they accept them, so keep trying. In addition to the following recipes, you can find some simple directions for home-blended baby food on Wholesome Baby Food's Web site (www.wholesomebabyfood.com).

RECIPES

For 6-month-olds

Pureed Yams or Sweet Potatoes

Bake a yam or sweet potato until tender.

Peel and toss into a blender or bowl.

Add ¼ cup water.

Blend or mix until the mixture is quite smooth and runs off the spoon. If the mixture is too thick or chunky, add more water and continue blending. For storage, pour into ice cube trays, freeze until solid, and then store in labeled freezer bags for up to six months.

Avocado Delight

Blend one ripe avocado with a bit of breast milk or organic formula.

Freeze in ice cube trays for easy storage and then dump into freezer bags.
The puree will keep for up to six months.

Banana Breast Milk Blend

Mash a ripe banana until smooth and blend in 4 tablespoons breast milk or
organic formula.

Freeze in ice cube trays and preserve in freezer bags for up to six months. Frozen leftover cubes will brown a bit, but baby will still gobble them down.

Eco-nomical Tip

Even making just a portion of baby's meals from scratch will save you money and planetary impact. Homemade purees cost much less than jarred food—and there are no containers to dispose of.

147

For 8- to 10-month-olds

Breakfast porridge

¼ cup oat flour (simply grind oats in blender or food processor)
4 tablespoons water
1 teaspoon vanilla extract
½ teaspoon ground flaxseeds

Put the ingredients in a microwave-safe bowl and zap for 30 seconds. Stir and check porridge to see if it needs slightly more cooking time. Make sure to cool before serving.

Autumn Vegetable Medley

1 cup baked sweet potato, peeled
1 cup baked winter squash, peeled
Enough breast milk or water to achieve desired consistency

1 cup applesauce or baked apple, peeled
½ teaspoon ground cinnamon

Blend all the ingredients until smooth. Pour some into ice cube trays and freeze. Keep cubes in a sealable bag for up to six months.

Pear Tofu Pudding

½ cup silken tofu
1 peeled, seeded pear

¼ teaspoon ground cinnamon
⅛ teaspoon ground nutmeg

Blend ingredients until smooth. This works best as a fresh food although you can experiment with freezing.

For 12-month-olds

Fruity Veggie Popsicles

Toss clean, cored organic fruits into the blender (see suggestions below).

Add spinach, cooked sweet potato, or another veggie of your choice.

Add organic juice or whole milk yogurt.

Blend, experimenting with the proportions until you like the flavor and consistency.

Pour into Popsicle molds or small cups with Popsicle sticks.

Freeze and serve.

Here are some examples you could try:

❁ Strawberries, spinach, and fruit juice

❁ Sliced oranges or mango with sweet potato and carrot

❁ Spinach, cucumber, and lemonade

149

BPA-Free Bottles, Sippy Cups, and Dinnerware

Many of the plastic bottles, baby plates, and spoons manufactured today contain Biphesenol-A (BPA), a component of plastic that has already been banned in Canada and Europe. When plastics are heated repeatedly, which we regularly do when washing dishes, the BPA leaches out into baby's food or milk. In lab rats, low-level exposure to BPA has been linked to obesity, diabetes, thyroid disease, and a few types of cancer. Check the resource guide at the end of the chapter for several recommendations on BPA-free bottles and dinnerware.

Pumpkin Pancakes

2 tablespoons vegetable oil or cooking spray

½ cup canned organic pumpkin puree (or bananas, sweet potatoes, or squash)

1 egg

¼ cup yogurt

3 tablespoons breast milk or whole milk

¾ cup flour

½ teaspoon baking powder

½ teaspoon ground cinnamon

Mix all moist ingredients in one bowl and dry ingredients in a separate bowl. Combine them, adding additional milk if needed to get to pourable consistency. Warm griddle or skillet to medium heat and coat with vegetable oil. Pour ¼ cup of batter for each pancake onto the pan and cook about three minutes on each side. Serve immediately, or freeze and store for up to one month. You can top with applesauce or pure maple syrup but these steaming cakes are fantastic with or without any additions.

Homemade Teething Biscuits

⅓ cup white flour

⅔ cup wheat flour

1 cup white grape or apple juice

1 cup baby cereal (oats, rice, or barley)

½ teaspoon ground cinnamon

1 teaspoon vanilla extract

Mix all ingredients. Sandwich the sticky dough between two sheets of waxed paper and pat until it's about ½ inch thick. Freeze the dough for about 10 minutes so that it becomes solid enough to peel the waxed paper away. Cut into rectangles and place on a well-greased cookie sheet. Bake at 350° F for 50 to 60 minutes. The cookies won't burn despite the long baking time and need to be quite firm to withstand baby's gnawing. Always be sure to supervise your child when providing teething biscuits and watch out for choking.

Plumping Baby Up

When Rebecca's pediatrician was worried about her daughter's slow weight gain, she recommended Pediasure, a processed nonorganic dairy product with artificial flavors, sugar, and maltodextrin. Ever the independent thinker, Rebecca resisted her advice and came up with a thriftier, eco-friendlier, and more natural solution. She found a variety of healthful, high-fat ingredients and slipped them into her daughter's morning porridge:

- Two tablespoons olive oil

- A few scoops of brown rice protein powder (available at natural foods stores)

- A few tablespoons of flax meal

- Almond meal or sunflower seed butter

- Pureed avocado

Rebecca met with a pediatric nutritionist, who applauded her efforts to fatten her baby naturally. After a month or two on this high-calorie diet, the pediatrician was pleased with Audrey's weight gain. If you do choose to fatten baby naturally, check with your pediatrician first.

151

Skipping Baby Food Altogether

As baby gets older, many parents opt to use a food processor, blender, or food mill to mash up whatever they're eating for dinner. There's no reason you can't dump a portion of spaghetti and marinara into the blender and let your eight-month-old enjoy the same flavors you're savoring at the dinner table. Parents need to watch sodium content and may want to toss in some breast milk or banana to moisten the mixture, but it's a great way for baby to feel included at mealtimes. You could even use a mini-food mill at restaurants or while traveling to blend up whatever is available at the time. It saves you the hassle of having to pack jarred food and then trying to find recycling centers on the go.

When Organic Baby Food Saves You Money

Think organic baby food is pricey? Gerber's Wagon Wheels are a common first finger food. They're made of corn and rice flour, sugar, and some other ingredients. But at $2.38 for a 1.48-ounce can, they end up costing more than $25.00 a pound! Compare that with organic puffs from Nature's Path or Arrowhead Mills. The only ingredient is the grain itself—rice, kamut, corn, or wheat. At $1.99 a bag, they cost about $5.30 a pound. So you save by going organic.

Here's another example: A 24-ounce jar of organic applesauce from Trader Joe's costs $2.29. You'd have to buy ten little baby food jars of conventional Beech Nut applesauce for the same amount, which would cost you $5.70. Not only would you pay more than twice as much for conventionally grown food, nine more jars would have to be manufactured (and recycled by you)—plus nine lids would go directly into the trash.

Organic Jarred Foods

The lesson that parenting seems to teach over and over again is *be flexible*. If you're planning on making every drop of baby food from scratch, be open to the fact that exhaustion may occasionally trump your plans. Or, if you think it's utterly impossible to make your own baby food, give it a whirl and see what you think. We cannot overemphasize just how easy it is to blend homemade baby food. Still, as working moms ourselves, we can certainly understand the need to sometimes buy jarred food as a time saving (and sanity saving) measure. The organic baby food market has exploded in recent years, offering a wide variety of options to parents.

Obviously the very cheapest and earth-friendliest organic baby food is prepared at home. If you don't have the time or inclination to whip up home-blended baby food, O Organics Safeway Baby Food is by far the least expensive, but it's only available at Safeway stores. Earth's Best can be purchased in bulk cases at stores like Costco for around $.28 an ounce, which also makes it a good value.

Organic Baby Foods: How Do They Compare?

	PRESERVATION PROCESS	COST PER OUNCE	AVAILABILITY	ENVIRONMENTAL CONSIDERATIONS
Organic Baby Food Prepared at Home	Fresh or frozen	$.10	Available everywhere!	No reason to have to throw anything away
O Organics/ Safeway Baby Food	Jarred	$.25	Available at Safeway stores	Glass jars can be recycled but lids cannot
Gerber Organics	Jarred	$.33	Widespread	Packaged in plastic— not recyclable in all areas
Earth's Best	Jarred	$.34	Widespread	Glass jars can be recycled but lids cannot
Happy Baby	Frozen in cubes	$.42	Somewhat widespread	Packaged in plastic— not recyclable in all areas
Pomme Bebe	Stored in refrigerated tubs	$.93	Limited	Packaged in plastic— not recyclable in all areas

153

Limiting Your Family's Meat Intake

Each pound of meat requires 2,500 gallons of water, compared with only 60 gallons of water to produce a pound of wheat. In addition to water usage, there is the issue of deforestation and land use, plus the pollution generated by animals raised for food. Following are a few options that you can think about as you set out to fill your baby with healthful, eco-friendly foods.

- **Cut back on meat—even a little bit.** Try to schedule a few meatless days per week and use meat as an ingredient in meals rather than a focus. It'll cut back your grocery bill, increase your consumption of fruits and veggies, and greatly limit your carbon footprint. You'll notice that your child will probably naturally lean toward the smooth texture of fruits and veggies in those early days. If you introduce baby to a diet with smaller quantities of meat early, it will be a seamless transition.

- **Buy organic, local meats.** If your family can't cut back on meats, try getting them locally from trusted sources. You'll avoid the environmental cost of raising and shipping meat across the country, and you'll feel good about knowing where your food is coming from.

- **Go vegetarian.** Vegetarians skip animal meat but still feast on eggs and dairy, along with grains and produce. As a vegetarian, you'll dramatically cut back on the cost of groceries, up your consumption of fruits and veggies, and potentially extend your life. If you're vegetarian and are worried about whether to embrace the lifestyle for your child, you can rest assured that there are many vegetarian children thriving around the world.

- **Go vegan.** Vegans avoid all animal products while enjoying the bounty of whole grains, vegetables, and fruits. Vegans are enjoying more variety on supermarket shelves than ever before. Tofu, tempeh, and other soy products that were formerly hard to find are now appearing even in small-town grocery stores.

Beyond the Baby Food Aisle

The best discovery the two of us made on prepared food was to think outside the baby food jar. We found that large containers of organic pureed applesauce, boxes of frozen organic sweet potatoes, and cans of organic pumpkin puree were quite a bit cheaper than official baby food and just as beneficial. As our children grew, we bought organic cereal puffs and sometimes organic canned beans for finger foods.

The Circle of Life:
From Food Scraps to Fertilizer

First it was the spaghetti. Joy's son Roscoe would pile heaps of noodles on his head at dinner and peek out from the pasta tendrils. Then he came up with another coy little trick for mealtimes: spitting out food. He popped it into his mouth, took a few chews to savor the taste, and then just as happily let it dribble down his chin while he went for the next bite. The family's meals involved lots of belly laughs, but they wondered what to do with all that wasted food.

Families with dogs don't ever have to ask themselves that question—and probably also have very clean floors. Since the only thing resembling pets in Joy's home are wilted houseplants, their family depends on the compost bin to function as a food waste controller. Rather than sending scraps to a landfill, where they don't have enough air to decompose properly, composting allows food to biodegrade and be reused as fertilizer. Joy keeps a plastic container (purchased at a thrift store) on their countertop and dumps in all the nondairy, nonmeat waste that ends up on Roscoe's tray at each meal. Then, they regularly head out to their Darth Vader–shaped compost bin and toss in the latest batch.

Over their years of composting, they've learned just how many things can be tossed in, including tea bags, manure from vegetarian animals, wood ashes, paper napkins, fall leaves, and grass clippings. Somehow the bin never fills up, no matter how many overflowing containers of scraps they load into it. Good old Darth manages to quickly digest them, leaving plenty of room for Roscoe's offerings.

For those that haven't started a compost bin yet, it's far simpler than you might guess. You can make your compost bin out of an old trash can and just a few other materials. After you rig up a composting system, you'll save on your garbage bill and prevent several hundred pounds of waste from heading to a landfill each year. Instead of sitting under layers of trash, your eggshells and orange peels will be producing rich soil that you can use in your garden next spring! Check the end of the chapter for a list of online composting resources.

In the spring when Joy's family pulls rich dirt out of the bin for use in their garden beds, they are glad that they trooped out into the rain all winter long to dump potato peels and carrot tops. That dirt manages to help them grow organic tomatoes, basil, and peppers for lovely summer meals that Roscoe will likely be putting on his head instead of into his mouth. Those scraps will again end up in the mouth of dear old Darth, the family's favorite compost bin.

Born with a Green Spoon in Their Mouth . . .

Armed with good information, healthful food, and a trust in your own instincts, you'll find that feeding your child quickly becomes a simple part of parenting. And while you're saving the planet, you can take heart in the fact that your eco-efforts are keeping nutritious food in baby's belly and thousands of dollars in your savings account.

Eco-nomical Tip

The average American tosses about 1,200 pounds of compostable waste into the trash can each year. With babies and toddlers, it often seems like half the meal has to be disposed of on a daily basis—adding to your trash bill and your eco-guilt. Starting a compost pile is a great way to produce free fertilizer and reduce garbage pickup costs.

Easy Composting for Apartment Dwellers and Gardeners Alike

Bokashi bins have revolutionized composting for people living in small spaces—and those that don't want to slog out to the backyard in the middle of winter with their food scraps. The other great benefit of these handy five-gallon indoor bins is that you can compost dairy, fish, meat, and animal bones along with your banana peels and strawberry hulls—all without unpleasant odors or worms! All it takes to activate this wondrous system is a sprinkle of bokashi—which is made up of water, wheat bran, molasses, and microbes that break food down quickly. Plus, you can drain the liquid runoff or "compost tea" using a spigot at the bottom of the bin and use it as a fertilizer on your houseplants or in a terrace garden. After just ten to fourteen days in the Bokashi bin, food waste turns into a "pre-compost product" that can go outside in the garden or on your balcony in potted plants. The creators recommend buying two bins. When one fills up, it should sit for one and a half to two weeks to break down while you dump fresh scraps in the other. Within one month of burying the "compost product" in soil, it will turn to nutrient-rich dirt. It's the perfect solution for toddlers who mix all their leftovers into a giant mush and for sleep-deprived parents who can conveniently dump that mess into the bin without having to tromp outside. Apartment dwellers can distribute the "precompost product" in house plants, bury it in balcony flowerpots, or give it to friends to use in their gardens.

Resources

Breastfeeding Resources

✿ **Womenshealth.gov** has detailed information about coping with breastfeeding challenges as well as a breastfeeding hotline open from 9 a.m. to 6 p.m. eastern time.

✿ Lactation consultants are hired by hospitals who know that investing in breast-feeding support will create healthier children in the long run. Check with your local hospital to contact a lactation consultant or check the **International Lactation Consultant Association** directory online (www.ilca.org.)

Milk and Food Storage Resources

✿ **Sensible Lines Milk Trays** (www.sensiblelines.com) freeze breast milk into long thin sticks that easily fit in any bottle opening. They're BPA-free and have been designed by moms for moms.

✿ **Baby Cubes** (www.babycubes.com) are BPA-free individual storage containers for breast milk or baby food that fit handily into freezer trays. They are microwave, dish-washer, and freezer safe and come in a variety of sizes.

Homemade Baby Food

✿ **Wholesomebabyfood.com** has a variety of great tips and suggestions for making your own food at home, as does **Homemade Baby Food Recipes.com.** (www.homemade-baby-food-recipes.com)

BPA-Free Bottles

Glass

✿ **Bornfree Glass Bottles** (www.newbornfree.com)

✿ **Evenflo Glass Bottles** (www.evenflo.com)

Plastic

⚙ **Avent Baby Botttles** (www.avent.com)

⚙ **Thinkbaby Bottles** (www.thinkbabybottles.com)

⚙ **Green to Grow Baby Bottles** (www.greentogrow.com)

⚙ **Nuby BPA Free Baby Bottles** (www.nuby.be)

BPA-Free Sippy Cups

⚙ **Thermos Foogo Sippy Cups** (www.thermos.com)

⚙ **Nuby Sippy Cups** (www.nuby.be)

⚙ **Avent Magic Sippy Cups** (www.avent.com)

⚙ **The Safe Sippy** (www.thesafesippy.com)

BPA-Free Dishes and Utensils

⚙ **Thinkbaby Stainless-Steel Feeding Set** (www.thinkbabybottles.com)

⚙ **Sassy Baby Feeding Set** (www.sassybaby.com)

8

Living Green
Despite the Obstacles:
Eco-friendly Tips
for Special Circumstances

What happens to your dreams of cloth diapering the minute you see two or even three babies on the ultrasound screen? Can a career-minded mom find an eco-friendly daycare and keep up with the demands of breastfeeding? What about balancing the rigors of single parenting with the challenge of green living? It's possible! But don't take our word for it. Throughout the chapter you'll find firsthand accounts of ingenious parents who are going green despite the obstacles.

Double Duty: Juggling Work and Baby

According to U.S. census data, 55 percent of women with infant children work outside the home—which means that more than half of us are struggling to meet the many demands of career and motherhood. Integrating our environmental ideals into this precarious balancing act can seem completely overwhelming. It isn't always easy, but it is manageable to have a sane work and family balance while going green. We both returned to our jobs just a few months after having our babies. As we reentered the workforce, sleep deprived and dazed, we realized what we could have done beforehand to make the transition easier. Keep reading to hear how we—and other eco-minded parents—found ways to achieve that elusive work-life-baby-environment balance.

Green Daycares: Do They Exist?

Unless your partner can stay home with the kids, the first challenge of balancing career with family is finding a childcare solution that fits your eco-sensibilities and your budget. If you opt to use cloth diapers but can't find a provider who's willing to work with you, your efforts may feel hardly worth the trouble. Here are a few steps for getting a jump on finding a green daycare for your child.

❦ **Think outside the box.** Do you have flex time at work that you can stretch to give you a few more hours a week with your children? Can you share a nanny with a few other sets of parents or ask extended family to pitch in with daycare one day a week? All these options are probably cheaper than daycare and may allow more flexibility with your green plans.

❦ **Get a jump start.** When Joy began searching for a daycare center in the eighth month of her pregnancy, she was shocked to learn that several of the most popular locations had waiting lists of more than a year! It's best to start interviewing daycare providers months before you'll ever need them, partially so that you'll find a good spot for your child but also so that you'll have some practice asking questions and evaluating centers.

Ask like-minded friends and family for referrals. The best sources for names are other green parents who adore their providers and can't stop raving about them. We've learned from experience that you should accept nothing less from your daycare.

Consider your questions. You'll want to have a list of them on hand with a note-pad for answers. The following questions address green living, but you'll also want to add your own inquiries about things like pets, television, smoking, and child-to-adult ratios.

1. **Are you willing to work with cloth diapers?** You might want to bring your dry bag and diapers to show the providers. Some have never seen the newer cloth diapers and don't realize how easy they are. Plus, slipping a cloth diaper into a dry bag isn't any harder than dumping a disposable in the trash. Rebecca's daycare provider had never worked with cloth before but was happy to try it out because it meant she had less trash to take out. Keep in mind that some of the larger centers might be limited by state sanitation requirements.

2. **Do you feed the children organic/vegetarian/other special food? If not, can I bring food for my child?**

3. **Are your sippy cups, bottles, and teethers BPA-free? If not, can I provide my own equipment for my child?** The two facilities Joy used provided bottles for her son. Rebecca brought along her own bottles to her daughter's home daycare.

4. **I'll be providing breast milk for my child during his/her time at daycare. Do you foresee any problems with that?** It's wise to figure out the daycare's policy about breast milk, as many state-run places have strict rules about how long a bottle can be left out before tossing the entire thing. It can be frustrating to pump sixteen ounces of milk only to learn they threw twelve ounces down the drain because your baby didn't drink it quickly enough. You may find it necessary to prepare several smaller bottles or freeze your milk in ice cube trays to avoid this scenario.

🎁 **Go with your gut.** Your instincts are the most important factor to consider when making a decision. If you get a few flutters of discomfort, keep looking. Joy's original daycare center came highly recommended, but it didn't feel right from the beginning. Her son was always screaming when she went to pick him up, he refused to drink the breast milk she so painstakingly pumped, and they wouldn't use cloth diapers. She opted to move him and ended up with an eco-friendly daycare that accepted cloth diapers, had him quickly gulping down breast milk from a bottle—and even turned out to be less expensive than the first center.

Balancing the Domestic Workload

Green living with baby does produce more household chores. It's critical that families share the burden so that one parent doesn't end up saddled with endless domestic duties on top of caring for baby and managing a career. Before your infant ever arrives, discuss household responsibilities and practice allocating chores. The early days of parenthood are quite stressful, as sleep deprivation eats away at your patience and productivity. Any practice you have now at comanaging cooking, cleaning, and other choices will be a great help in the long run.

Joy went back to work just six weeks after her first child was born, which turned out to be borderline insane. While the sleep deprivation was humbling, they did all right with housework because she and her husband had each established realms of responsibility that complemented each other. For example, he handles all laundry (including cloth diapers) whereas she does all the meal planning and cooking. Joy pays bills, and he makes sure recycling, garbage and compost all get where they need to be on time.

It can be especially difficult to balance chores if one parent has an extended leave from work while the other parent's schedule continues as normal. Three months later, the stay-at-home parent returns to the workforce and finds she is still doing most of the household tasks as well. It's helpful to discuss your roles both during and after a maternity or paternity leave.

True Pumping Tales

These moms managed to pump despite challenging circumstances but found it to be well worth it in the end.

"I traveled for work when we had our first daughter. I spent the first ten months after maternity leave pumping. I have pumped in every place you can imagine. I've pumped at rest areas, airports, hotels, restaurants, office bathrooms (thousands of them), and countless other places. I flew almost every week and would have to fight with the security check people . . . when it came to carrying on my pump and bag full of milk in a cooler. They would always take my bags completely apart.

"Most people thought that I was nuts for continuing to breastfeed my daughter. However, I felt like even if I was away from home for a couple days she always had a little bit of me with her to comfort her. When she was sick she had my healthy milk to help her heal. In the end I think that it was as much for me as it was for her.

"I would fight airport security every day all over again if I had to. It was worth it for both of us."

EMILY LAH, St. Joseph, Michigan

"With our first baby I was so nutty about pumping; I'd do it up to three times a day at work . . . making sure I matched ounce for ounce what he drank every day while I was away. I was kind of a wreck about it. With our second baby, I'm a lot more relaxed about it. I only pump once before I leave for work in the morning and once around noon at work.

"We gave him some formula a couple times just after I came back to work, just so if we did have to at some point it wouldn't be the devastating event I'd envisioned in my mind. He drank it a bit—didn't really like it—but survived the ordeal (as did I) and we've not needed to supplement so far (he's eight months old now).

"I'm reminded every day by news articles sharing the health benefits of breast-feeding for both baby and mama, supportive friends and family, and that goofy milk-drunk look I get from my sweet boy that it's worth all the effort!"

KARA LESTER, Springfield, Oregon

Pumping 9 to 5:
Breastfeeding as a Working Mother

For many women, breastfeeding is a challenge in the early weeks but gets easier as time goes on. Women who work outside the home, however, find the challenge becomes greater when their maternity leave ends and they suddenly have to find time to pump in the midst of career demands. How can you have a productive and private experience with pumping at work? If possible, start planning while pregnant.

❦ **Find a pumping place.** According to laws in most states, employers have to provide a private, sanitary area for you to pump your breast milk (and that doesn't include a bathroom stall). See about using a locked office, a small kitchen, or a conference room. Check for outlets nearby and a surface for setting up the pump. Also, find out if there's refrigeration available at your workplace or if you need to pack a cooler to take to work with you.

❦ **Think about scheduling pumping.** If you work at a breakneck pace all day, you'll need to think about finding a few thirty-minute windows of time to pump during the workday. The less you pump, the less supply you'll generate, so think frequency instead of just duration. Working mothers often find ways to multitask, but be careful; stress will prevent your milk from flowing.

❦ **Ask other working moms for tips.** No one understands the demands of pumping at work like those who have been there. They'll give you ideas about where to go, who to ask, and possibly even help you find time in your schedule for pumping. Use all the help that you're offered, because chances are you'll need it!

Going Green with a Resistant Spouse

Are you thrilled about using cloth diapers and breastfeeding, while your spouse is set on Pampers and powdered formula? Many parents rely on old-school family advice when it comes to raising baby and aren't comfortable trying something new with their infant. If your spouse is such a person, fear not! It's possible to get him or her on board as part of an eco-friendly team. Joy's advice (from experience) is to do the research together and give your spouse a chance to talk to other parents who have successfully incorporated green choices into their lives with baby.

Joy's Experience: How I Got My Husband to Go Green

My husband loves hiking, polar bears, native plants, and organic cherry tomatoes. We met on Earth Day at an eco-friendly volunteer event and share a deep appreciation for the natural world. Why then does he turn the thermostat up to seventy-one degrees while loafing around the house in shorts and a T-shirt? Why does he drive to the park with our son when he, an avid marathoner, could push the stroller there in a mere ten minutes? Sadly, I think I know the answer to my own questions. My husband, the love of my life, is a lazy environmentalist.

I enjoy my marriage to this wonderful, supportive, and nurturing man who can sometimes fall into the role of an eco-slacker. The good news is that, like most of us, he's highly resistant to change until he's taken the first small steps successfully—at which point he'll jump on the bandwagon and be there to stay. Now he's the one who launders cloth diapers more than I do. Composting seemed a bit messy to him, but he has transformed into a diligent waste manager as he willingly takes out our apple peels and radish tops on a daily basis.

I've found that it's best to endure the grumbling and forge ahead with small changes until my husband becomes more of a leader than a follower. I still sometimes wish that he would internalize the impact of carbon emissions and take initiative without prompting, but after knowing and loving him for a long time, I realize that he's a status quo kind of guy who needs a little eco-nudging now and then.

Cloth Diapering in a Laundromat

Is it possible? Absolutely! Is it cheaper than disposables? Yes! Even if you have to pay to run the washer and dryer, you can save money using cloth diapers. As long as your washer and dryer work reasonably well and you don't have to keep feeding it quarters to ensure your load comes out clean, it should be a better choice for the environment, too. We're basing our calculations on a $1 fee for running the washer and another $1 for the dryer (note: these costs may double in bigger cities). Obviously a family could save money and carbon emissions by hanging diapers to dry, but that not may be practical in an apartment.

If you wash diapers every four days, or ninety times a year, and can run one cycle per load without extra rinses, plus one cycle in the dryer, you'll pay $180 per year on diaper laundry in a coin-operated machine. If you use Biokleen Laundry detergent (which we've found to be the most cost-effective green detergent), you'll spend $.139/load, or $12.51/year on detergent for diaper loads. **Total washing and drying costs (for one year): $192.51.**

The startup costs for cloth diapers will run you between $120 and $600, but since *Consumer Reports* estimates you'll spend between $600 and $800 annually on disposables, you'll still come out ahead using a coin-operated laundry. Plus, keep in mind that even if you do start cloth diapering and give up, you can usually sell back your diapers and get as much as half your money back.

As for the practical side of washing cloth diapers in an apartment, it's up to you to decide if you're willing to lug an odorous diaper pail down to the public laundry facilities. If your laundry room is private enough or you are courageous enough not to care, your pocketbook and the planet will benefit!

Double Trouble?
Cloth Diapering with Twins

Talk about obstacles! Many parents might be shocked to learn that cloth diapering with multiples is quite possible and sometimes even more convenient than using disposables. Furthermore, the money you'll save by cloth diapering will be substantial, and every bit counts when you're raising more than one baby on a budget. Diaper services will often offer discounts for parents of multiples, and you may get some deals by buying your supplies in large quantities. Also consider asking for help from friends and family as you stock your cloth diaper layette and prepare for the whirlwind of babies about to enter your home.

Emily Aderhold switched to cloth diapers for her twins at four months, not just because of the expense but because of environmental and health concerns. In the long run, she found that using cloth was actually *more* convenient than disposable diapering. Although many people would admire her efforts, she's rather humble about cloth diapering her twins, and finds that it's not as hard as most people think. We interviewed her to find out just how she managed to thrive while cloth diapering multiple babies.

Eco-nomical Baby Guide: How many diapers do you use a day, and how many would you recommend a family buy for diapering twins?

Emily: We go through about twenty-four diapers in a twenty-four-hour period. We have about forty diapers total, and about twelve covers. I would recommend buying a few of each kind of diaper to see what fits your family's lifestyle the best: prefold, fitted, pocket, all-in-one pocket, before splurging on your whole stash.

While doing Internet research, we would have gone with all fitteds and all-in-ones, but when we actually had them in our house and were using them, we found we liked the old-fashioned prefolds the best. If you have a lot of help from friends and family, or a reluctant spouse, you may want to buy some cloth diapers that are self-explanatory. You may not be able to expect a babysitter to figure out how to put on a prefold (though it isn't hard).

EBG: What inspired you to switch to cloth diapers with two babies?

Emily: To save money, create less waste, and for the health of our children. The fact that there are chemicals in disposable diapers that have been banned from feminine hygiene products is startling. I want the safest things for my children, and I want them to live in a clean world when they are having children of their own.

EBG: Do you feel cloth diapers are more work than disposables since you've had a chance to try both of them on your twins?

Emily: Not at all! The thing I hate about doing laundry is folding and putting it in the different drawers and closets. But diaper laundry is simple. Disposable diapers require more work in my opinion. I'd have to notice we're running low, go to the store, spend hard-earned money on something that is only going to hold waste and go in the trash then the landfill, and walk the stinky diapers out to the trash bin. I found that to be more work and a big blow to my green conscience.

EBG: What are the hidden conveniences of using cloth diapers with twins?

Emily: Every family is different, but we don't leave the house to run errands with our twins. We enjoy going to someone's house, but not running in and out of stores. Having all my diapering supplies from four months (when we started using cloth) until they hit thirty pounds, at my home, ready to go, is so much more convenient.

EBG: How much money do you estimate you've saved by cloth diapering?

Emily: The first four months of their lives, we were spending about $100 a month on diapers, buying a less expensive brand of disposables. When we switched to cloth, we spent about $400. So, the first four months of using cloth, we were breaking even. Every month after that, we are saving $100. When they outgrow their diapers or covers, I can resell them or give them to a family in need. If I sell them, I will use that money to buy the next size up. I estimate that we will spend about $100 when we size up (this will be in well over a year).

EBG: How should expectant parents of twins handle the skepticism that they might get when others hear that they're planning on using cloth?

Emily: I have not had any skepticism. Or maybe I have but just closed my ears to it! We do a lot of natural, green things for the babies. My husband and I want them to be happy and healthy and give them the best start we can. Mostly people just want to know all about it. Diapers are so different than they were years ago, and people are amazed at how much easier it is now than when they were diapering their children. I think, too, that when you have multiples, people expect you to always take the "easy" way out, and when you step up and do something else, they are really more in awe of you than skeptical.

Preparing for Your Adopted Child

As our world population skyrockets and the strain on our environment grows, adoption is becoming increasingly attractive as a way to support a child, complete a family, and help the planet. But how do you prepare for a baby when gender and age are unknowns? How can friends and family support you with a baby shower when some factors are a mystery?

171

Wait to buy. Although it's tempting to purchase clothes and toys in anticipation of your arrival, remember that there's no way to predict exactly what your child needs until you are holding him or her in your arms. If you have food, a few blankets, and some diapers on hand, you'll do just fine.

Mobilize your support team. Inform friends and family that they'll be sent out on errands in the first few days to gather up anything you might need. Consider asking for a shower after your child arrives so that you'll have a better idea of what you'll need. Also, appoint a friend or family member to send out a group e-mail listing everything you'll need and then let him or her coordinate the contributions. Give yourself plenty of time to just adjust to parenthood.

Adoptive Baby Shower Tip

"I gave some input to my sisters-in-law. I wanted a focus on my daughter and her birth country. She was born in Ethiopia, and there it is tradition to name children because of the meaning. My daughter's name means 'my light.' Instead of playing typical shower games, we played a game on Ethiopian trivia. I also gave people the option of donating to a charitable organization rather than giving me a material gift."

DEEANN NORD

Single Green Parenting

According to the U.S. Census Bureau, a quarter of all families with children under the age of six are being raised by single parents. While we bow before the feet of all single parents because of their tremendous skills and workload, we realize the first practical hurdle they face is financial. Single parents earning more than $40,000 a year will spend about a third of their annual income on their child, whereas dual-income families earning the same amount will spend just 23 percent of their yearly earnings on a child.

So how can single-parent families cut costs while trying to go green? Reusing, recycling, and buying less are the best ways for parents to radically reduce planetary impact while slashing costs at the same time. Buying used clothing and gear will allow a parent to cut the baby budget by more than 80 percent, helping increase financial security and limit the need to work extra hours.

Since single parents have to shoulder more domestic responsibilities in addition to their career demands, it's critical that they ask for help from a circle of support. Especially in those first few weeks, single parents shouldn't hesitate to ask friends to deliver casseroles, provide free child care, and don rubber gloves for a house cleaning or two. Asking for help will save your sanity and get you some much-deserved rest.

But buying used and getting support doesn't address all the challenges of eco-friendly single parenting. To find out how single parents in the trenches are thriving and surviving while going green, we turned to Eileen Spillman, a single mother of two who manages to work full time as a middle school math teacher and raise her children while considering the planet.

Eco-nomical Baby Guide: Why do you choose to live green despite the other demands on your time as a single parent?

Eileen: It just doesn't feel optional to me. We are in a state of crisis with our environment, and we either need to all change our lifestyles drastically or seriously research life on the moon. How can we *not* at least try to make greener choices?

EBG: How do you handle the economic challenges of single parenting and eco-friendly living?

Eileen: Truly eco-friendly living means not buying things new and reducing consumption all around. So for me, eco-friendly living saves me money. I shop at thrift stores, save on utility bills, save on cleaning supplies, spend less on gas. There is no reason to spend a lot of money on an eco-friendly lifestyle.

EBG: What are the top five things you use to limit planetary impact in your household?

Eileen:

1. We stopped using paper products like napkins, paper towels, etc. Instead we use all-cloth napkins and rags. Instead of rolls of paper towels around the house, I now have cloth bags filled with rags, and I added a hamper in my kitchen.

2. I switched all of my lightbulbs to compact fluorescent.

3. During the summer, I didn't use my clothes dryer unless absolutely necessary.

4. I use all homemade cleaning products now. The main ingredients in most are baking soda and vinegar, which are safe for my family and for the fishies.

5. We try to limit car trips as much as possible and often manage car-free weekends. During the week I carpool a few days a week. Even just two days a week of carpooling makes a huge difference.

EBG: Many single parents want to do more, but struggle with green guilt. What would you tell them?

Eileen: The first thing I would tell a single parent is to cut yourself some slack and don't try to reinvent your entire lifestyle overnight. Start with one change and add it in gradually. When you've mastered that, think about the next thing. The lightbulbs, for instance, are an easy change. Just buy a pack of fluorescent bulbs, and as your bulbs go out, replace them. Same with paper towels. I think it's okay to feel guilty and, in fact, we *should* feel guilty for wasting resources. Just don't allow the guilt to turn into anxiety, and try not to overwhelm yourself with too many changes all at once.

EBG: How have you made changes in your lifestyle in the midst of your busy schedule?

Eileen: I didn't do a lifestyle makeover, I just had a shift in mind-set, and over the course of about a year, I had made most of the big changes. None of them were costly or time-consuming, and I didn't throw anything out to get started, I just would replace things with more green options as they were used up. I am not done! I would say that finding ways to reduce and conserve has provided me a much-needed creative outlet. Trying to find new and better ways to reduce and conserve, figuring out how to repair things instead of replace, or finding the perfect item to fit a need have become a fun hobby for me.

Progress, Not Perfection

If you've read this book all the way through, you've heard this message again and again: Green parenting is about progress, not perfection! We don't expect everyone to expertly navigate the challenges of eco-parenting despite the obstacles, but it's nice to know that there are simple ways of moving toward greener living even in difficult circumstances. The parents in this chapter have shown that it is possible to take small steps toward eco-friendly living without overextending your budget or your sanity.

CHAPTER

9

Ten Simple Things You Can
Do for the Planet Right Now
(and Four Difficult Ones)

You may have heard this depressing statistic: North Americans comprise just 5 percent of the globe's population but use 25 percent of the world's resources. Our lifestyles have turned parenthood into an industry like anything else. Still, it is possible to reduce our ecological footprints while preparing to bring a new life into the world—without depriving your child or adding to your already busy schedule.

For those of us taking everything one baby step at a time, this chapter contains ten simple things you can try. And for those who've mastered the little things and want to go even further, we've mused on four more difficult lifestyle changes that could make a big difference to Mother Earth.

Ten Simple Things You Can Do for the Planet Right Now

We really can save the planet, one compact fluorescent lightbulb at a time. Okay, while one lightbulb won't put an end to global warming, there are hundreds of small steps you can take to "green" your life with a new baby—and the more people that jump on the green bandwagon, the better.

Number 1: RECHARGE THOSE BATTERIES

With around three billion batteries sold each year, their disposal is taking a big toll on the planet. Every one you pop into a children's toy, swing, or vibrating bouncy seat contains heavy metals such as mercury, lead, cadmium, and nickel. How do you get rid of them? If you toss them in the trash, they'll probably go to a landfill. The metals in the batteries pollute our water systems and leach out of our landfills, contaminating our planet with lead and acid.

Many parents find themselves using more batteries than ever as they buy battery-operated contraptions and toys for their new babies. What's the solution? **Don't buy them!** Remember that parents and children all around the world survive without dolls that light up, sing songs, and teach baby the colors of the rainbow.

That said, we realize that you may end up with some of these gizmos. Here are our tips:

❦ **Battery rechargers are a good option** for parents who have many battery-operated devices.

❦ **Look for plug-in versions of power-operated devices.** The Fisher Price Power Plus Swing plugs in instead of relying on battery power.

❦ **Swings and vibrating bouncy seats that take batteries can be converted to use electricity** with a universal DC battery eliminator available at electronics stores and places like Target.

❦ If you use regular batteries, **recycle them**! Places like Radio Shack collect dead batteries. While they may not actually recycle them, they will turn them in to a hazardous waste facility rather than send them to a landfill, where they will do environmental damage.

❦ Some contraptions such as swings work at varying speeds, play music, and light up. **The fewer features you use, the longer your batteries will last.**

Number 2: PAINT IT GREEN

Redecorating your baby's nursery? Plan on painting those walls a soothing green or vibrant orange? Traditional paints contain volatile organic compounds (VOCs), which are chemicals that are released during and after painting. These chemicals have been linked to maladies such as headaches, dizziness, asthma, and even cancer.

Don't panic—it's easy to find low-VOC paints that are water- rather than petroleum-based. If you really want to avoid VOCs, look for paints with a "zero-VOC" label. Clay paint, milk paint, and lime washes are also natural alternatives to conventional paints.

No- or Low-VOC paint brands worth checking out include Benjamin Moore's Aura, Yolo Colorhouse, and Oympic Premium.

Number 3: TURN DOWN THE HEAT

In Rebecca's newborn care class, she learned that it was best to keep thermostats set at 72 degrees for a baby's comfort. This was quite a blow to someone who had been keeping her house at a chilly 62 degrees to do her part for the environment! Keeping your house too warm can do a number on your pocketbook, not to mention the environment.

So what's an eco-conscious new parent to do? First of all, remember that overheating and overbundling a baby have more serious risks (increased SIDS risk) than exposing your newborn to slightly lower temperatures. You know baby is too hot when he's red and sweaty. If his little hands and feet are freezing, you know he'd appreciate another layer of clothing.

Nowadays Rebecca keeps her house at 64 degrees during the day and her daughter runs around with hardly a stitch on. Like her mother, she is content to live in a cooler house! Here are some ideas that will help you nudge that thermostat down:

🎁 **Don't heat what you don't use.** If you want baby to stay extra warm, you can heat up his room with a space heater and keep the rest of the house cooler.

🎁 **Bundle up.** You don't need to forgo comfort to save the planet. Just throw on an extra layer and snuggle baby into a warm blanket. Turn your thermostat down just one degree, and you can slash your energy usage by 3 percent. Decrease your overall house temperature by 1 degree each week to adjust gradually. Setting your thermostat just 2 degrees lower over the course of a year will save 2,000 pounds in carbon dioxide emissions.

🎁 **Crank it down when you're gone.** You may have fallen prey to the myth that it takes more energy to heat up a cold house than to leave the heat running. Wrong! Turning the heat down while away from home or sleeping *always* saves energy.

🎁 **Insulate.** Believe it or not, good insulation makes more of a difference than having solar panels on your home. It's the least expensive and most effective thing you can do to save energy. Many local utility companies will do energy audits to check whether your home is well insulated.

Number 4: THROW AN ECO-BIRTHDAY BASH

Plastic goodie bags stuffed with cheap toys, piles of presents wrapped in gaudy paper, store-bought cupcakes on decorative paper plates . . . is all this expense and waste really necessary? Here are a few tips to keep your birthday parties a little more down-to-earth and earth-friendly:

🎁 **Ditch disposables.** This goes for plates, plastic forks, invitations, and decorations. Try online options such as Evites instead of paper invitations, and look for decorations that can be used year after year. Not up to washing piles of dishes crusted in frosting? Go for disposable plates made from recycled materials. Chinet's plates are made from 100 percent recycled materials and can go in the compost bin when you're done. While not as exciting as Disney-themed plates, they're much kinder on the planet.

🎁 **Green your gifts.** A gift-free party is the best way to avoid waste—both from toys your child doesn't need and wrapping paper that goes straight into the trash. If you don't want to go that far, try suggesting a book-themed party or even a used-toy swap in lieu of traditional presents. Wrap your child's presents in reusable gift bags. Joy owns a whole collection of fabric gift bags tied with ribbons that she brings out for every special occasion.

🎁 **Go for greener goodies.** Instead of giving out plastic bags filled with throwaway items, have the children make a craft during the party that they take home. Or buck the social norms and don't give in to the goodie bag trend. When your babies are little and most of the guests are adults, most people won't be sad to go home without a useless party favor!

Number 5: CHECK IT OUT . . . GO TO THE LIBRARY

Here's a sad story: We know an excited grandmother-to-be who saw a deal she couldn't refuse: a complete set of Disney movies at a discount price. She snapped up the entire collection, thrilled that she'd be able to give it to her grandchildren one day. The only problem was, her daughter wasn't actually pregnant at the time. Years went by, and eventually she got the grandchild she'd always wanted. Unfortunately, by now everyone was into some newfangled technology known as DVDs. And the entire Disney collection was in VHS. Whoops.

Okay, that was an extreme example, but the fact is, kids do eventually outgrow their piles of Baby Einstein DVDs, then the Dora the Explorer phase, then the Disney collection, and on and on. Then there are the books: How many children's books become childhood favorites, and how many get nothing but a disdainful glance before they're tossed in the charity pile?

181

Low-Pressure, Low-Impact Birthday Parties from Real Moms

"I don't feel too pressured when planning a party for my kids, because they are so young—they really don't know what they are missing with regard to those cheap party trinkets. They just want to make sure they get a cake! I did buy some decorations for my firstborn's first birthday party, but I saved what I could for when my second child turned one. Perhaps it will become more of an issue when the kids are older, and maybe then I will feel more pressure.

"I try not to get swept up in all the hullabaloo. . . .So far, most of my kids' parties have involved more adults than children (not too many of our friends have kids!) so I don't rent bouncy tents and trained monkeys that ride around on bicycles or anything like that. I try to remember that the birthday is for the child, not the parents."

VANESSA MACLEOD, Beaverton, Oregon

"For Jane's birthday, in June, we always went up to Mt. Tabor park and had a picnic with friends and family. We'd make fried chicken and pasta salad and have strawberry shortcake. No gifts (from party goers—she'd get gifts at home from family) and no major party theme. Because she has a birthday that does not fall during the school year, it has been no big deal, and she never seemed to notice that she didn't have a fairy princess birthday party.

"For school, we also are grateful that parties tend to be lowkey. People often rent the (private) school gym for parties, which is cheap, and kids can run around like crazy. You need to invite everyone in their class if you are using the school to deliver invitations. You bring your own food and minimize waste and garbage."

ANNA WHITE, Portland, Oregon

182

The cheap, eco-friendly solution is to make good use of your library. The Multnomah County Library system in Portland, Oregon, has every children's DVD, book on tape, and plain old book you could ever want. Rebecca admits to keeping some books and DVDs checked out for *more than a year* if her daughter takes to one. If no other parents have requested the items, this is perfectly legit.

You may assume that your library does not carry many DVDs when you look at the shelves. The trick is to look up the titles you want in the online catalog; most likely they are simply checked out. Place holds on the movies and books you want, and they'll show up. The Multnomah County library allows patrons to put fifteen titles on hold at a time. When you keep your queue filled at all times, you can have a constant collection of movies and books streaming in (and then out) of your house—without a Netflix subscription! Some libraries such as the Seattle library allow up to one hundred holds at a time.

Rebecca and her husband used the library for pregnancy books, parenting books, sleep solution books, a hypno-birthing tutorial, regular cookbooks, baby food cookbooks, DVDs of HBO and Showtime series, and endless movies to watch during maternity leave. These would have cost hundreds of dollars, and most of them aren't the kind of thing you'd need to keep around after your baby enters toddlerhood.

Number 6: SAY IT WITH FLOWERS (AND PLANTS)

When you're expecting a new baby, you may start to worry about the air quality in your home. You may even start testing for lead, asbestos, and other contaminants. You might want to purchase an air purifier to make sure baby breathes in nothing but the best. While it's great to think about your indoor air quality, sometimes there's a fine line between "greening" your house and becoming completely paranoid.

Here's an easy way to purify the air in your house and absorb some of those pesky carbon emissions: get some houseplants. In the 1980s, a NASA study determined that houseplants can help remove common household toxins such as trichloroethylene, benzene, and formaldehyde from your home. According to *Your Naturally Healthy Home* by Alan Berman, these ten plants do the best job at zapping pollutants and toxins and counteracting greenhouse gases:

- Areca palm
- Boston fern
- Australian sword fern
- Weeping fig
- Reed palm
- Janet Craig dracaena
- Peace Lily
- Dwarf date palm
- English ivy
- Rubber plant

Number 7: SWITCH TO RENEWABLE ENERGY

Did you know that the average family uses 25 percent more energy once a baby enters the home? They do more loads of laundry, run a few extra baths, and crank up the heat. Check with your service provider and see if it's possible to sign up for renewable energy. If it's available to you, it's easy to access your account online, make the switch, and pay just a dollar or two more each month. When you sign on to support renewable energy, you're helping fund projects that create green energy sources.

Number 8: DON'T THROW OUT THE BATHWATER (OR THE BABY)

Is a daily bath really necessary? Many parents find they can simplify their routine by bathing their babies less frequently. Rebecca's daughter enjoys weekly baths and appears no worse for the wear—plus she's keeping more than six thousand gallons of water from going down the drain every year. Think, too, of the energy it takes to heat all that water. Remember that it's better for baby's skin to reduce exposure to water and bath products. (Pediatricians usually recommend avoiding all bath products until babies are at least six weeks old. Just plain water will do.)

Joy, on the other hand, has integrated nightly baths into her son's routine but has some tricks up her sleeve for "recycling" her bathwater:

❁ If you have a top loader, transfer bathwater to the washing machine for a load of laundry.

❁ Collect the water in buckets and use it in the garden (make sure you are using all pure and natural bath products).

❁ Use bathwater to do any pre-soaking of dirty clothes. Joy washes out diaper covers in the bathwater after her son is out of the tub.

❁ Shower or bathe with the baby.

✱ Use a baby bathtub or the kitchen sink. If you can find a used baby bathtub, this may be one hunk of plastic that will save at least fifteen gallons of water per bath.

✱ Use the bathwater to flush toilets. However, don't leave a bath full of water if your baby is mobile and able to climb into the bath while you're not looking!

✱ If you want to get really serious about reusing your gray water, look into Brac Systems—a Canadian company that recovers bathwater and redirects it for use in toilets. They claim you can save 40 percent of your water costs.

Number 9: CLEANER AND GREENER

Television advertising might lead you to believe that germs are lurking on every surface of your house, ready to strike you dead at any moment. These ads are filled with concerned moms who spend all day ridding the shower of soap scum, the floor of "harmful bacteria," and the toilet from deadly diseases. It's no wonder the average family shells out more than $600 per year on household cleaning products.

The great irony is all this scrubbing and scouring can actually be harming your health—and the health of the environment. Neither of us spends even close to $600 a year on cleaning products (more like under $50!), and everyone in our families has lived to tell about it.

A few greener cleaning ideas:

✱ **Rethink "clean."** You may feel like a new baby needs a perfectly sanitized environment, but in reality the toxic commercial products could be adversely affecting the air quality in your home. Second and third children as well as children in daycare have much healthier immune systems than their more sheltered counterparts. Allergies have recently skyrocketed in developed countries, leading scientists to develop the "hygiene hypothesis." It's based on research showing links between extremely clean environments and increased risks for allergies and asthma, possibly because more sterile environments create weaker immune systems. So, before you feel compelled to clean every speck of dust off the floor, remember having a spotless house isn't necessarily best for your child.

✿ **Keep out the dirt.** Taking your shoes off before you enter the house can help keep your floors free from grime.

✿ **Make your own cleaning solutions.** Common pantry items such as vinegar, baking soda, and borax are just a few of the inexpensive ingredients you can use to clean your house. Visit oeconline.org for a list of homemade cleaning recipes you can easily whip up yourself for just pennies.

✿ **Buy greener cleaners.** Don't want to make your own concoctions? Try brands like Seventh Generation, Method, and Biokleen, which avoid chlorine, phosphates, and other ingredients that can be bad for your health and the environment.

So You Want to Switch—What Do You Do with Your Nongreen Cleaners?

You have a few options:

- ❧ **Slowly use them up** and replace them with nontoxic cleaners as they run out.
- ❧ If worry about your family's health causes you to want an immediate transition, **drop them off at a hazardous waste facility**.
- ❧ **Give them away.** If others are going to buy these products anyway, this is actually an eco-friendly idea. At least you're keeping them from buying one more bottle.
- ❧ What about **flushing them down the toilet**? This not only wastes water, it contaminates our water supply. Let the experts deal with it.

Number 10: HOW MANY SLEEP-DEPRIVED PARENTS DOES IT TAKE TO CHANGE A LIGHTBULB?

When you're getting up at all hours of the night, you may reach for the light switch more than you care to count. You may as well be using a lightbulb that saves electricity. The

Union of Concerned Scientists projects that 90 billion pounds of greenhouse gases could be spared if every American family replaced just one regular bulb with a compact fluorescent bulb! Compact fluorescent bulbs cost more at first but end up saving more than $30 in energy costs by the time they burn out because they last up to ten times longer. Because the bulbs contain mercury, it's important to recycle them somewhere like Home Depot when they've expired.

Four More Difficult Things You Can Do to Save the Planet

While taking baby steps toward greenness can be rewarding—not to mention manageable on limited sleep—sometimes we can lose focus on the big picture. Are we patting our backs for changing a lightbulb when we should be doing even more to save the planet? The purpose of this section is not to make you feel like all the little things you *are* doing don't amount to anything. We firmly believe that every little bit counts. It all starts with changing a lightbulb . . . but where can you go from there?

Number 1: LIMIT FAMILY SIZE OR ADOPT

Mention anything about limiting family size to save the planet and you'll get some interesting reactions, ranging from shocked to dismissive. Perhaps because of China's one-child policy, the very idea of limiting the number of children we bring into the world takes on dictatorial overtones. In some religions, doing anything to prevent a child from being born is blasphemy. At the other end of the spectrum are a handful of environmentalists who believe having even one child is a selfish act that will destroy our planet.

So why are we even touching this issue in *The Eco-nomical Baby Guide*? Well, there may be some of you who have a child and are on the fence about a second. Barring any religious imperative to populate the Earth, it might be useful to weigh the environmental pros and cons to having a child in addition to all the other factors. And of course, there is a way to have a large family without bringing another biological child into the world: adoption.

While limited resources may not be the first reason to expand your family through adoption, it is a way to stick to the ol' "zero population growth" credo.

Number 2: STAY PUT OR DOWNSIZE

The number one expense you'll encounter as a new parent isn't diapers or daycare: It's housing. The USDA estimates that a third of your child-rearing expenses will go to the roof over your head. Families in large Western cities—the most expensive places to live in the United States—will spend 10 percent more. While rural families will spend 7 percent less than urban dwellers, their savings will be offset by higher transportation and medical expenses.

According to the National Association of Home Builders, the average house size in 1950 was just 953 square feet—and families were much bigger back then! By 1970, the average house size was up to 1,500 square feet, and by 1990 the size jumped to more than 2,000.

How do smaller homes help the environment? It takes half the amount of energy to heat Joy's 1,000-square-foot house than the average 2,349-square-foot American dwelling. Live in an apartment with under 600 square feet? Even better—you'll use a quarter of the energy the average home does.

Both of us chose location over house size—so owning a smaller house means we can walk to shopping, parks, work, public transportation, and school. Joy's savings in taxes, commuting, energy consumption, and house payments have allowed her to cut back on work hours to spend more time with her family. And because they live in the city, Rebecca has never had to own a car.

You'll also find that the square footage of your home will dictate how much baby gear you are able to acquire. You won't need a baby monitor in a small house, and you simply won't have room for a play gym, bouncy seat, *and* a bassinet. As Joy says, "We don't buy it unless we're willing to trip over it."

Number 3: SAVE A COW—GO VEGETARIAN

Is it possible to have a healthy pregnancy and baby on a vegetarian diet? Naturally! Rebecca has been a vegetarian since her early teens, and she and her noncarnivorous husband are raising their daughter vegetarian. They rarely spend more than $175 a month on groceries, and that includes organic produce. Compare that to a three-person family on the USDA's "thrifty plan": they spend $414.20. In addition, vegetarians enjoy one or two extra years of life and spend less on healthcare.

Aside from health and frugality, going vegetarian is a great way to go green. Livestock (and the grain to feed livestock) takes up a whopping 30 percent of our land's surface, taking over what used to be wilderness and Amazon rainforests.[12] Most of us are aware that cars are big polluters—livestock creates 18 percent more greenhouse gases than all of our transportation methods put together!

The average American eats two hundred pounds of meat each year. A family of four spends about $2,300 annually on meat ($192 a month), and that number is climbing.[13] Families can afford to eat more meat than previous generations, but that luxury takes a toll on the planet. Many Americans are jumping into the green movement—recycling more, driving less. Eating lower on the food chain is another simple thing you can do to help out Mother Earth. If everyone cut down their animal protein intake by 10 percent, we could feed all the hungry people of the world with the grain saved.[14]

Now, for some, going vegetarian would be a major sacrifice. The good news is, even part-time vegetarianism helps conserve resources. If your family eats vegetarian just one day, you could save eighteen *thousand* gallons of water—that's what it takes to produce one pound of raw beef! Go to www.meatlessmondays.com for information on part-time vegetarianism.

[12] According to a 2006 report published by the United Nations Food and Agriculture Organization.

[13] According to the U.S. Department of Agriculture and Bureau of Labor Statistics.

[14] According to www.earthsave.org.

Little Baby, Big Impact

In April 2008, *Mother Jones* listed some startling statistics in their article "What's Your Baby's Carbon Footprint?" Here are some of the highlights:

- What frightens 60 percent of kids in the United States more than cancer, terrorism, or automobile accidents? **Global warming.**

- In a fifty-year span, 1.2 billion children will be born in Africa compared with just 114 million in the United States, yet each group will generate the same amount of **carbon emissions.**

- One hundred and six Haitian children produce the same amount of **carbon dioxide** as just one youngster in the USA.

- Only 2 percent of Indian babies and 6 percent of Chinese babies wear **disposable diapers**, compared with 96 percent of U.S. babies.

Number 4: CAREFREE & CAR FREE

The reality is that cars have become indispensible to a suburban lifestyle. Rows and rows of single-family houses can be miles away from schools, libraries, gyms, and grocery stores. Getting rid of one car—let alone two—would require a major lifestyle change for many Americans.

While many expecting parents move to the suburbs to accommodate their expanding families, others are staying in the city or moving *in*to the city to live a greener life. With an urban lifestyle often comes smaller living spaces and less reliance on cars. Instead, parents walk their kids to school, do their errands by foot, and take the bus or subway to get where they need to go.

How much do you spend each year on just one car? The cost of the car itself, the price of insurance and maintenance, and the constant gas fill-ups can really add up. The average car drives 12,000 miles each year. If your car gets 20 miles per gallon, that's 600 gallons of gas. Get rid of one—or two—cars and the planet will thank you.

Going Car Free

BY ANGELA AND DOREA VIERLING-CLAASSEN

The summer we met culminated in a cross-country trip from Boston to Nebraska. We fell in love while passing the miles in a tiny truck and cooking our breakfasts and lunches on its engine. We crossed the country again the next summer, and this time the truck had high plywood walls painted with orange, red, and blue flames and held all of Dorea's worldly possessions. We loved that truck like a member of the family. However, in the fall of 2004, shortly after we were married, the truck let us down; its clutch went out while we were living in the suburbs, seven miles from both of our workplaces. Being cheapskates, we decided not to replace or repair it. Instead, we shed the gas guzzler and learned to live without it, doing our grocery shopping by bus and commuting by bike and commuter rail. When we moved back into the city about a month later, we decided that if we could do it in the suburbs, we could easily live without a car in the city; we decided to become permanently car free.

When we were expecting our first child in 2006, people asked, "When are you going to get a car?" We would confidently reply, "We're planning on staying car free," which would usually result in a rueful chuckle, "Oh, we'll see how long that lasts—having a baby changes everything." When our daughter was born at a hospital three blocks from our home, we did not bring a car seat, but the hospital wouldn't let us leave without seeing her strapped in, even if she had no car to get into. We called a friend to bring us an infant seat, strapped the baby in, and carried her outside. We then put Angela, exhausted from labor, into a cab along with the empty car seat. Dorea walked home with our new baby nestled in her arms, as that seemed much safer than trying to puzzle out the cryptic car seat installation. Even in an urban area, where many people live without their own cars, being car free with a baby makes you a little strange.

Now, with another baby on the way, we feel more committed than ever to enjoying our family life without the hassle of car ownership. In the past two years as a car-free family (four as a car-free couple), we have learned a lot about what works for us. Along the way, we have made some key decisions that made our lifestyle workable. It's not necessarily an easy transition, but if you can take the leap you'll find that it gets easier and more rewarding with each passing month.

❧ When we bought our condo, we looked for something within easy walking distance to **public transportation** and one of our jobs. Because housing is very costly in the city, we chose to live in a smaller space, rather than to buy more than we could afford.

continued

191

Going Car Free (continued)

- ❦ We choose to **do almost everything locally**, even when potentially "better" options exist further from home. Day care, schools, doctors, libraries, playgroups, parks, restaurants, and even a swimming pool can all be found less than a mile from our home. By sticking to our local neighborhood, we minimize transportation time and get better connected to our neighbors and community institutions.

- ❦ **We bike**, which gives us more freedom than relying solely on public transportation and walking, and gives us exercise as well. It's also more risky, so you have to weigh benefits and risks, particularly when biking with children. We feel comfortable riding with our toddler in a bike seat both in our neighborhood and along bike paths.

- ❦ We look forward to the day when **our children can transport themselves** to school and activities in our neighborhood by foot. Also, our children will be able to take public transportation independently well before they would be allowed to drive on their own.

- ❦ We get our **groceries by bike** from a very affordable store two miles away, or by foot or subway from a closer (but more expensive) grocery when the weather is unpleasant. We carry them home in a rolling cart or in bike panniers. We purchased an extended frame bike (an Xtracycle) both for child transportation and to make grocery shopping and other chores easier.

- ❦ We utilize a **carsharing service** (ours is called Zipcar) that ensures that we can have access to a car any time we need it. We use the car rarely, perhaps six to ten times a year, often going several months without getting behind the wheel.

We have found that there are enormous benefits to being car free beyond the obvious financial perks, but many of them are subtle. We have wonderful friends nearby that we might not otherwise have found. We feel like we belong to a strong community and have many opportunities to interact spontaneously with the people that live in our neighborhood. Our world has gotten smaller in a way that feels comfortable and welcoming. We get far more exercise through walking and biking that we would if we were car owners, especially given the time demands of our jobs and family responsibilities. Above all, we are happy to be teaching our daughter about our values—community, sustainability, and environmental stewardship—through our most basic everyday activities.

Angela and Dorea Vierling-Claassen blog about their car-free adventures in Cambridge, Massachusetts, at www.carfreewithkids.blogspot.com.

Baby Steps and Large Strides toward Greenness

Whether you're living off the grid on a soybean farm or just screwing in your first compact fluorescent lightbulb, the green movement has a place for you and your new addition. You may find, as we do, that eco-nomical living does not involve much sacrifice and drudgery. Simmering your own organic applesauce on the stove, creating baby wipes out of old T-shirts, and walking your baby to the library aren't just activities you do for the environment—they're almost . . . well, *fun*. Plus, cutting back on consumption and focusing on relationships isn't just budget friendly and eco-friendly, it's a great recipe for a connected family.

Resources

⚙ **Oregon Environmental Council** (www.oeconline.org) offers a printable fold-out card containing recipes for a window cleaner, a wood cleaner, an all-purpose cleaner, and many others.

⚙ *Your Naturally Healthy Home* by Alan Berman has more tips on ridding your house of toxins.

⚙ **Brac Systems** (www.bracsystems.com) is a Canadian company that's designed a system for recycling gray water in household toilets.

⚙ **Meatless Mondays** (www.meatlessmonday.com) offers recipes, statistics, and inspiration for those wanting to skip meat at least one day of the week.

193

Index

Published in 2010 by Stewart, Tabori & Chang
An imprint of ABRAMS

Library of Congress Cataloging-in-Publication Data:

Hatch, Joy.
The eco-nomical baby guide : down-to-earth ways for parents to save money and the planet /
Joy Hatch and Rebecca Kelley.
p. cm.
Includes index.
ISBN 978-1-58479-831-6
1. Green movement. 2. Infants—Care—Environmental aspects. 3. Parenting—Environmental aspects. 4. Environmentalism.
I. Kelley, Rebecca. II. Title.
GE195.K44 2010
649'.1—dc22
2009014523

Editor **Dervla Kelly**
Designer **woolypear**
Production Manager **Tina Cameron**

The text of this book was composed in Baskerville, Gotham, and Oxtail.

Printed and bound in China

10 9 8 7 6 5 4 3 2 1

ABRAMS
THE ART OF BOOKS SINCE 1949

115 West 18th Street
New York, NY 10011
www.abramsbooks.com